"This devotional goes far be[ ] and resurrection of Christ [ ] truths. They are the framework of our identity. Our hope for change. Anna and Katy don't speak for God but instead provide readers with a way to intimately engage God Himself through daily readings, personal reflection, and prayer."

—**Julie Sparkman**, counselor, coauthor of *Unhitching from the Crazy Train*

"Katy and Anna have offered us a great gift. If you are looking for a beautiful, thoughtful, and wise companion to guide you through Lent and into Easter, you have definitely found one in *Easter Matters*."

—**Jim Branch**, director of Core Leadership; author of *The Blue Book: A Devotional Guide for Every Season of Your Life*

"It is an honor to recommend *Easter Matters: How the Resurrection of Jesus Changes You*, a devotional that tells the story of the life and death of Jesus Christ as recorded in the book of John. Jesus lived and died so that we might have eternal life, and this is what matters. Katy and Anna have done a great job of presenting the facts and truth in a practical and applicable manner. Thank you, Katy and Anna, for sharing with us this important perspective during the Easter season."

—**Mary Glynn Peeples**, author of *All We Like Sheep*; *Parenting, an Heir Raising Experience*; *Abounding Hope*; and *A Notebook for the Rest of Your Life*

"*Easter Matters* bridges the gap between the historical retelling of Jesus' death and resurrection and our personal stories of coming alive in Christ today. Offering powerful tools of beautifully crafted prayer, eternal promises, and the practical how-to of processing these truths in our everyday lives, this book is sure to transform the reader for His glory."

—**Amy Elaine Martinez**, former radio show host, founder of Amy Elaine Ministries, author of *Becoming a Victory Girl*

"With *Easter Matters*, Anna Nash and Katy Shelton have created a fun and engaging devotional that invites us all to sit at Jesus' feet as we prepare our hearts for Easter. Laced with biblical promises and helpful questions, this little book will inspire you, challenge you, and encourage you. But most of all, it will draw you deeper into the Father's arms."

—**John Greco**, author, *The Ascent: A Devotional Adventure Through the Book of Psalms,* co-owner of GTB Editorial, proprietor of pagesofjoy.com

"What do our heavy hearts and broken world need most right now? The hope of Jesus and eternal life that we celebrate on Easter! In *Easter Matters*, Anna Nash and Katy Shelton offer a compelling and spiritually rich guide that makes it easy to imagine walking beside Jesus and builds anticipation for the most important day of the year. Whether you read this devotional during the forty days of Lent or when you long to hear God's promises, it will change you and remind you that you are seen, cherished, and unconditionally loved."

—**Kari Kampakis**, best-selling author of *Love Her Well* and host of *The Girl Mom* podcast

Easter Matters

HOW THE RESURRECTION OF JESUS CHANGES YOU

AN EASTER DEVOTIONAL

ANNA NASH *and* KATY SHELTON

IRON STREAM

Birmingham, Alabama

Easter Matters: How the Resurrection of Jesus Changes You

Iron Stream Media
100 Missionary Ridge
Birmingham, AL 35242
IronStreamMedia.com

Library of Congress Control Number: 2021948576

A previous edition of this book was produced and sold by SCWC Books, a division of the Southern Christian Writers Conference.
www.southernchristianwriters.com

ISBN: 978-1-56309-546-7 paperback
ISBN: 978-1-56309-547-4 eBook

1 2 3 4 5—26 25 24 23 22
Printed in the United States of America

For Tyler and John
who also believe that Jesus changes us

Contents

Note to the Reader

We have always been friends. We played dolls together as little girls, we tried out for cheerleading together as teenagers, and we were there for each other on our wedding days. We grew up together, enjoying our similarities and learning to appreciate our differences.

As adults, we have been through celebrations and disappointments together. Over time, we have laughed and laughed and laughed, and yes, we have also cried. Just like everyone, our lives have been full of both good times and bad.

Although we have always been friends, there was a point in our friendship when things changed. In a surprising turn and at a surprising age—fifty something—we discovered a new type of relationship: a working friendship. In faith, we set out on a new adventure together, attempting to create something that might become meaningful. This journey, consisting of collaboration, hard work, and high hopes, began our unexpected new chapter. We put our heads together and, prayerfully, began to write.

The idea of writing a Christmas devotional based on the Gospel of Luke, we hoped, was only the beginning. Together, combining Katy's love for writing with Anna's love for ministering to others, we embarked on this new journey and began to envision and formulate the idea of future collaborative projects. Our desire to follow *Christmas Matters: How the Birth of Jesus Makes a Difference Every Day* with an Easter devotional based on the Gospel of John soon moved from our heads and hearts into our laptops.

This is how *Easter Matters: How the Resurrection of Jesus Changes You* came to be written. In writing this book, our greatest desire is simply to help others focus on our Savior, the Messiah, during the Easter season and beyond.

How to Use This Book

Like *Christmas Matters*, this book is intended as a guide or supplement to a gospel account of Jesus's ministry on earth. It in no way encompasses every detail of the Gospel of John, but rather it is intended to bring focus to significant truths about who we are as we personally relate to Christ.

In the Bible's New Testament, the fourth gospel—which follows the books of Matthew, Mark, and Luke—introduces Jesus through the eyes of His beloved disciple, John. In *Easter Matters* we will spend the forty-day Lenten season, which begins on Ash Wednesday and ends the Thursday before Easter, exploring the twenty-one chapters in the Gospel of John. As we discover how Jesus related to those around Him, we will see pictures of how He relates to us.

You might want to begin reading this devotional on Ash Wednesday, but you may prefer to begin reading on Palm Sunday, during Holy Week, or even on Easter Sunday. The story of Jesus told in the Gospel of John has the power to change your life no matter when you decide to begin celebrating His resurrection.

In this devotional, each chapter of John is divided into two days of reflection. On the first day, we will read content related to the correlating chapter in John, learning about and drawing encouragement from Jesus's life. This day will begin with an overview verse from the chapter in John and end with a verse containing a promise, reminding us of the freedom and reward found when we see ourselves as God sees us.

On the second day, each chapter provides the opportunity to personally process the truths about Jesus and how His birth, life, death, and resurrection change us. These interactive readings include the following:

- A process including questions to help you personally apply what you've read
- A prayer that provides an opportunity to move into conversation with God, talking and listening to Him. These prayers simply open the door for you to begin a meaningful dialogue with Him
- A few promises from the Bible reminding you of your new identity as a beloved son or daughter of our Creator and King

We ask that as you join us on this journey, you also read the chapter in John upon which each chapter in our book is based. John's words and account of Jesus are powerful, and reading them will bring context and clarity throughout the Easter season. The purpose of John is expressed in the concluding verse of chapter 20: "But these are written so that you may believe that Jesus is the Christ, the Son of God, and that by believing you may have life in his name." We echo these words written by John, and in faith, we wholeheartedly believe that the resurrection of Jesus will change you.

Anna and Katy

Introduction

I hear tiny feet pitter-patter across a polished wooden floor. It's Easter morning and the sun is rising. "There's *another* one!" my three-year-old son exclaims with delight, racing toward a baby-blue egg hidden in a corner of the room. His eyes widen as he opens the plastic egg, revealing a small piece of candy, a treasure. He tastes the sugary treat and a smile lights up his face. A moment later, his chubby hands clutch the handle of a basket filled with eggs, and my precious boy is off again, eagerly searching the room for more.

Easter. What a monumental day. This is the day we celebrate the resurrection of God's Son. On this day, we have reason to proclaim our new identity in Him, because of what He did for us. When He rose from the dead, everything changed. Beginning with this single moment in time, our new life was made possible.

Jesus's resurrection confirmed and affirmed an identity in us that cannot be shaken.

As we dig into the Easter story and its astonishing conclusion, you might find it hard to believe. Or you might believe the story, but it has become overly familiar. Or maybe you've never before heard the story. Regardless, what we will discover about Jesus is intense. It's horrible and it's wonderful. But most importantly, it opens the possibility for a new identity—one based upon how God sees us rather than how we might see ourselves. Our imperfections are replaced by His perfection, our sin by His righteousness. As we dive deep into the life of Jesus according to John, we will begin to understand what He has done for us. In each

d treasures—messages of love, notes of care,
rity. We will recognize our status as children
vill rest with assurance in new and powerful
s's tender message defines us not only on Easter
day of every year.

The narrative about Jesus found in the book of John enables us to turn our eyes toward Him and focus on His birth, His life, and His resurrection. John paints a picture of how Jesus interacted with the people surrounding Him during His time on earth, giving us insight into how He relates to and loves us. Because of who we are as children of God, we are privileged to "draw near" to Him, and in turn, He promises to "draw near" to us (James 4:8). As we get to know Jesus in the book of John, we will begin to have a clearer understanding of who He created us to be.

The journey ahead will give you a new perspective. You might find it difficult to see yourself as God sees you. Perhaps you are considering believing in Him for the very first time. Or possibly you have always believed in God but never truly experienced a relationship with Him. You may be a seasoned believer who desires a renewed sense of joy during the Easter celebration. Whichever is true, this beautiful and profound book of John is for you.

As we read through John's account of Jesus's life, we will be searching for and discovering new treasures every day. Like my young son on Easter morning, we will be filled with delight as these new treasures and truths unfold before us. In each chapter we will come face-to-face with Jesus, who came to make us complete. We invite you to join us on this forty-three-day journey as we prayerfully read through the book of John. You might be surprised or even disturbed by some of the events, but ultimately, what you find will be sweet and lovely and comforting.

Understanding and belief in the riches of God's love for us will provide the opportunity for a new life in Christ, filled with both security and freedom. This opportunity will nurture our souls and condition us for the most important celebration of the year: the celebration of His resurrection. Just as the earth shook and the stone rolled away on that glorious resurrection day, let's pray together that the stones of our doubt will also roll away. As we explore why Easter really does matter, we will discover amazing treasures that reveal how the resurrection of Jesus changes everything.

John 1

Seen, Part 1

Jesus answered him, "Before Philip called you, when you were under the fig tree, I saw you."

—John 1:48

Have you ever taken a morning walk at dawn and felt the promise of a new day? You see the piercing beams of light from beyond the horizon before you see the sun. These beams provide evidence that the sun will rise and the day will begin. You know it's coming. You know that at any second the bright sun will burst forth, almost blinding you. In a few seconds' time, predictably, the beams are replaced by full light and everything comes to life.

As we open the book of John and begin to read about the life of Jesus, we are reminded of light versus darkness. The people had been waiting in darkness for four hundred years, waiting for a savior to rescue them. The metaphorical darkness of mankind covered the earth as its people searched for light. But the promise of a savior allowed God's people to hope. They hoped that the prophecies would be fulfilled concerning sin and forgiveness, sickness and healing, death and life. The prophet Isaiah in chapter 61 declares a restoration that was coming, and the brokenness repaired. It was as if they could see the sunrise before they actually saw the sun.

The Gospel of John opens with God reaching down through the darkness to provide light for His children. "The true light, which gives light to everyone, was coming into the world" (v. 9). The true light, Jesus, was described as The Word. God's Word to His people was a gift of love, sacrifice, and restoration given in the person of Jesus. "For from his fullness we have all received, grace upon grace" (v. 16). This was the message from God to man. Hope would become reality and finally there would be a way for man to personally connect with God. "And the Word became flesh and dwelt among us, and we have seen his glory, glory as of the only Son from the Father, full of grace and truth" (v. 14). We will begin to better understand Jesus, God's gift to us, as we walk through the book of John page by page, story by story, truth by truth.

At times confusing, the book of John begins as we meet another John. John the Baptist, not the author of this gospel, is sometimes known as John the Baptizer. This John was sent to declare the message of Jesus's upcoming entrance into the world. His message clearly explained that God's people were about to receive the promised gift of the Messiah. Hopeful anticipation began to stir from village to village. What exactly was John the Baptist's proclamation? He said, "Behold, the Lamb of God, who takes away the sin of the world!" (v. 29). Sometimes God reassures His people with a tangible affirmation or sign. Here His "Holy Spirit descended on [Jesus] in bodily form, like a dove" (Luke 3:22) and rested on Jesus's shoulder, as if to say, "You can believe. This is My Son." The author goes on, "And John bore witness: 'I saw the Spirit descend from heaven like a dove, and it remained on him'" (v. 32).

After Jesus was baptized by John the Baptist, His short ministry on earth began. John, the author, tells us how Jesus began to choose His twelve disciples, those who would walk alongside Him as friends, coworkers, and carriers of the message of truth.

Each time Jesus chose a disciple—beginning with Andrew, his brother Simon (whom Jesus renamed Peter), and Philip—we see a similar pattern. He humbly engaged with them, extending an open invitation for them to follow along. And they did, without question. It's almost as if they could not resist Him. Whether it was belief in Him as the Chosen One of God or simple curiosity, they hoped for and wanted to find out more. Jesus journeyed through the streets looking for and seeing each disciple, calling them by name to join Him.

But the most intriguing invitation might be the one He extended to Nathanael. Philip, having decided to follow Jesus, went to find his friend. As they returned, "Jesus saw Nathanael coming toward him" and referred to him as "an Israelite . . . in whom there is no deceit" (v. 47). Nathanael—likely surprised—asked Jesus how He knew him, and Jesus replied, "Before Philip called you, when you were under the fig tree, I saw you" (v. 49). So Jesus saw Nathanael before Philip found him (v. 48), leading us to conclude that Jesus had a supernatural ability to see in a way humans cannot. Jesus not only saw him when Philip could not, but Jesus noticed him and recognized him as a man of impeccable character. Can you imagine what must have been going through Nathanael's mind? What must it have felt like to not only be seen by the Messiah but also to be regarded so highly? Surely it made him feel special, honored, and important. The light was shining upon Philip and Nathanael, preparing them to relate to God in a new way.

Years ago we took a family vacation to a large theme park. As the mom of four young children, I began to wonder how to keep my kids safe in the crowds of people. I decided to dress them in the same color T-shirts, one color for each day. I was constantly counting four little red, green, or blue T-shirts throughout each day of our vacation.

On yellow day, my worst nightmare came true. My daughter disappeared into the enormous sea of people. Yellow, yellow, yellow, where was that fourth yellow T-shirt? I had no idea so many terrible thoughts could go through my mind in such a short period of time. Finally, we saw her. Her little yellow self was standing on her toes trying to see above the crowd. She, too, was looking for us. It seemed like hours before we found her, but in reality it was only about fifteen minutes. There are no words to describe the relief when we found our precious one.

As the Bible tells us, you and I are *seen* by God. No matter what we are going through, no matter how alone we feel, God is with us. Darkness may at times overwhelm, and we may sometimes feel lost and separated from God, but by trusting in Him, we will begin to see evidence that He is near. His beams of light will ultimately overcome. Search for Him with confidence. Embrace the fact that He sees you, loves you, and will protect you. And when you press through darkness, be assured that you will ultimately find His light.

Promise
Light is sown for the righteous, and joy for the upright in heart. (Psalm 97:11)

John 1
Seen, Part 2

John 1 paints a picture of God's people. They had been waiting in spiritual darkness for four hundred years, waiting for their Messiah. The Gospel of John opens with a message of hope as we see God reaching down through the darkness to provide light for His children. The beams of light that we see before the sun rises provide evidence that the day will surely begin. Like these first beams of daylight, Jesus came to light the world, just as John the Baptist foretold. We, too, in our own lives can believe that Jesus will light our way and save us. If we believe, we can be assured that the light will burst forth, giving us unexplainable peace and hope. Our faith enables us to see that the first beams will be replaced by full light, and everything will look different in a moment's time. Hope lies in this moment.

Process

1. How do you personally connect with God? When was the last time you experienced this connection?
2. Do you believe that you can better understand Jesus through the eyes of John?
3. Can you think of a time recently or in the past when you did not feel seen or valued? Conversely, do you remember a time you felt highly valued?
4. How do you think Nathanael felt when Jesus said, "I saw you"?

5.   Why does it sometimes feel so difficult to receive Jesus's invitation to follow Him?

Prayer

God, thank You for the promise of a Savior. The gift of Your Son gives me daily hope. May I, like the people in the first chapter of John, believe that the prophecies will be fulfilled concerning sin and forgiveness, sickness and healing, death and life. Give my life the restoration it needs. Show me how my broken places will be repaired by You. Help me believe. Allow me to have hope that Your light is near. Through Your power, may I have the ability to walk by faith even when I cannot clearly see. Show me Your light piercing the darkness. When I feel overwhelmed, and sometimes lost and separated from You, remind me that You are always near and that You see me. I want to relate to You in a new, more intimate way today.

Promises

Draw near to God, and he will draw near to you. (James 4:8)

Behold, I stand at the door and knock. If anyone hears my voice and opens the door, I will come in to him and eat with him, and he with me. (Revelation 3:20)

Fear not, for I have redeemed you; I have called you by name, you are mine. (Isaiah 43:1)

Again, Jesus spoke to them, saying, "I am the light of the world. Whoever follows me will never walk in darkness, but will have the light of life." (John 8:12)

John 2
Priceless, Part 1

Now when he was in Jerusalem at the Passover Feast, many believed in his name when they saw the signs that he was doing.

—John 2:23

We were in the midst of the pandemic of 2020. As we had become accustomed during this time, my husband and I set the table outside in order to keep ourselves and our guests safe. That fall evening the stars shone beautifully. The firepit crackled, the candles burned brightly, and the aroma escaping the grill was heavenly. We excitedly welcomed our guests, keeping in mind the necessary precautions. Our friends had offered to bring a special bottle of wine for the four of us to enjoy. But when they used the word *special*, we had no idea how truly special it was!

As we uncorked the wine, they began to tell us its story. You see, our friends had not purchased this wonderful wine; it had been given to them. One day, out of the blue, they received a phone call from a local liquor store that their order had come in. But they had not placed an order. When our friend went to this store, he found a case of a wine he had not ordered with his name on it. After a few questions, he found there had been an error in the distribution process. When he tried to return the wine to its rightful owner, he was told, "We really don't care for that wine, so if you'd like, please keep it." A little more research revealed that

7

this was an expensive wine, much finer than our friends might have ever purchased. So there we sat under the stars enjoying our simple home-cooked meal paired with one of the finest wines we'd ever enjoyed. Feeling grateful, we made a special toast to one another and the unexpected gift.

As we embark on our journey through the Gospel of John, we begin with a similar story, a story about Jesus's first miracle on earth. On this day, Jesus, His family, and His disciples attended a wedding feast where the wine ran out before the celebration ended. When Jesus's mother made Him aware of this problem, He told the servants to fill six stone jars—used for the Jewish rites of purification—with water. He then told them to draw some out and take it to the master of the feast. The master, who had no idea Jesus was involved, immediately commented on the high quality of the wine. Jesus had not only turned water into wine but had also turned it into the finest of wine. We read that this sign, this unexpected gift, this first miracle, "manifested his glory" (v. 11).

It would not be long before the people would realize that Jesus often turned religious customs upside down. Here we see Jesus filling plain water jars with fine wine. Maybe Jesus wanted to make the point that a person's outer appearance is not always indicative of what's inside. Maybe He wanted to encourage us to focus on our hearts and minds first, rather than our actions. We sometimes try to perform for or impress others with charitable or religious activities, but maybe He is saying, "Just come and be with Me and enjoy all that I have to offer." Isaiah 55:1 says, "Come, everyone who thirsts, come to the waters; and he who has no money, come, buy and eat! Come, buy wine and milk without money and without price."

Following the miracle at the wedding, there is a second, quite different story and picture of Jesus. Passover was at hand, and Jesus went to the temple in Jerusalem to celebrate. Upon His arrival, He found the people had set up a market inside the temple, where animals were being traded and sold. While in the temple, His zeal rose to the surface. With great passion, energy, and probably anger, He turned over the tables, sending coins flying in every direction and animals running loose. His motivation? To keep the temple—His Father's house—from being turned into a market. As Jesus said in Matthew 10:34, "I have not come to bring peace, but a sword."

Sometimes, the purposes for which God sent His Son to earth brought division. The religious leaders inquired of Him, "What sign do you show us for doing these things?" (v. 18). His reply? "Destroy this temple, and in three days I will raise it up" (v. 19). "Impossible," they said. Of course, they didn't understand this foreshadowing. They didn't understand that the reference to the destruction of the temple represented His death and resurrection. And they didn't understand that it wouldn't be long before these sacrificial animals would no longer be needed. The ultimate sacrifice was forthcoming. To them, moving away from religious rituals toward a personal relationship with God was counterintuitive. They could not fathom what was about to happen.

The power of God was exhibited through the miracle at the wedding and the zeal of Jesus at the temple. In both instances, His powerful presence surely was felt by those around Him. His actions spoke loudly. Jesus was preparing the people. He was about to take their sin and turn it into holiness. He was about to metaphorically clean house. He would take their uncleanliness and turn it into holiness as a result of His sacrifice on the cross.

During Jesus's life, what He said and did on earth always had deep meaning. The people would soon understand the purposes of Jesus's death and resurrection and how these purposes would make a difference in who they were as His *priceless* children. As we begin to look beyond the surface of Jesus's life, we will begin to understand its significance. Just as God's people were being prepared for a new way of relating to Him, let us prepare our hearts to understand more clearly how priceless we are to Him.

Promise

They shall be mine, says the LORD of hosts, in the day when I make up my treasured possession, and I will spare them as a man spares his son who serves him. (Malachi 3:17)

John 2
Priceless, Part 2

Why does a gift feel so much more valuable than something you've purchased for yourself? The gift of grace is exactly like that. Its value offers provision for our souls that far surpasses anything we could ever buy for ourselves. Jesus's first miracle depicts love and grace, not only for the people at the wedding in Cana but for us as well. He used a priceless gift—the miracle of creating fine wine out of water—to bless the wedding guests. In doing so, He communicated that He cared and wanted to provide for His friends. He had a way of welcoming people without judging them. He saw every human being as important, and He had come to offer a new way for them to feel valuable.

Process
1. How are you tempted to live out your faith in a ceremonial or non-relational way?
2. In what ways do you live your life to perform or impress others?
3. Consider how the resurrection of Jesus offers you an opportunity to feel more valued in a way that you've never known.
4. Describe how grace feels.
5. What is one area of life where you need to experience God's grace right now?

Prayer

God, turn over my heart like Jesus turned over the tables. Show me any areas where I may be looking to other things for my worth. Make Your power known in my life more today than ever before. Help me to understand and be impacted by Your Son's death on the cross. This Easter, may I embrace all of Your gracious gifts for which I have done nothing to deserve. Thank You so much for the opportunity to be adopted as Your child and welcomed into Your kingdom. May I live today as if I belong to You and remember that I have great worth in Your eyes. Please help me to overcome my desire to find worth in earthly things and relationships.

Promises

Everyone who is called by my name,
   whom I created for my glory,
   whom I formed and made. (Isaiah 43:7)

Behold, I have engraved you on the palms of my hands;
   your walls are continually before me. (Isaiah 49:16)

He who did not spare his own Son but gave him up for us all, how will he not also with him graciously give us all things? (Romans 8:32)

In him we have redemption through his blood, the forgiveness of our trespasses, according to the riches of his grace. (Ephesians 1:7)

Even as he chose us in him before the foundation of the world, that we should be holy and blameless before him. (Ephesians 1:4)

John 3

New, Part 1

The Father loves the Son and has given all things into
his hand.

—John 3:35

Not long ago, I was mindlessly walking down the aisle at our local grocery store when my phone rang. It was my oldest son. "Mom, can we talk about my baptism and why you and dad made the choices for me that you did?" His question jolted me. But at the same time, I wasn't really surprised. This wonderful son of ours has never been one to take things at face value. He usually feels the need to understand why. He likes to question things until he fully understands the reasoning behind a thought, a word, or an action. And while I wasn't surprised, I'll never forget that moment, that question he posed, when I was in the middle of the grocery store. It challenged me in a new way. It challenged me to really think about baptism like I hadn't before. My husband and I had inherited a strong foundation of belief from our parents and our church. Now it was time to dig a little deeper and search our hearts and God's Word for further understanding of this sacrament that is so important in our Christian faith.

In an effort to organize my thoughts and explain them to my son, I found a wonderful explanation about baptism. Baptism is said to be not just an act of obedience but also an act of joyful expression. It celebrates a life committed to Christ. The water represents a washing in God's Holy Spirit. Many pastors, as they immerse or sprinkle someone with water, say something like this: "Based upon your profession of faith in the Lord Jesus Christ, I now baptize you in the name of the Father and the Son and the Holy Spirit. Buried with Him in the likeness of His death, and raised with Him in the likeness of His resurrection to walk in the newness of life."

Newness of life is the theme of John 3. In this chapter we find arguably the most famous scripture in all of the Bible—John 3:16: "For God so loved the world, that he gave his only Son, that whoever believes in him should not perish but have eternal life." People plaster this verse everywhere. From billboards and posters at athletic events to license plates, these are only a few examples that illustrate the popularity of this verse. But why is this particular verse so popular and so well known? John 3:16 summarizes the theme of the entire Bible in one clear, simple sentence. It's a writer's dream come true. Many have sought to discover who originally came up with this most famous verse in the Bible. Some say it was John since this is John's narrative. Others say it was Jesus since we often find Him speaking about Himself to others in third person. Personally, I like to think it was Jesus. I love the thought of Him speaking those words. It becomes personal and inviting. For God so loved *me*. If *I* believe in Him, *I* will not perish, but have life! How exciting to think of Jesus speaking directly to me! Today, let's look at the one to whom Jesus might have said these familiar words.

Nicodemus was his name. We are told he was "a ruler of the Jews" (v. 1). He came to Jerusalem by night, maybe in secret, to find Jesus. Nicodemus probably had hoped that Jesus was the Messiah, but he also must have had doubts, questioning the validity of this young leader who had gained such a large following. We read about Nicodemus in verse 2: "This man came to Jesus by night and said to him, 'Rabbi, we know that you are a teacher come from God, for no one can do these signs that you do unless God is with him.'" It's as if he were saying, "I want to believe, but I needed to meet you face-to-face to be sure."

Jesus often spoke in a challenging kind of way, causing people to think beyond religion toward a personal relationship with God. He wanted people to not only have a knowledge of God but also to have a belief in Him. He explained that they must be "born again" in order to "see the kingdom of God" (v. 3). Nicodemus, who must have been a literal thinker, asked Jesus how a person could reenter the womb to be born again. Jesus clarified that it was a rebirth of the soul, not the body. The way to have a spiritual birth, Jesus continued, was by believing. Belief in God and His Son, Jesus, was and is a cornerstone of the Christian faith. Jesus went on to reiterate the importance of belief, and in fact, belief is mentioned ten different times in this one chapter.

After Jesus's conversation with Nicodemus about new life, John the Baptizer reappeared in the story. John and Jesus were busy baptizing people in and around the Judean countryside, when a discussion arose between some of John's disciples and a particular Jewish man about the matter of ceremonial washing (v. 25). The group commented to John about Jesus, saying, "Look, he is baptizing, and all are going to him" (v. 26). It was if they were asking him if Jesus was qualified to administer this spiritual cleansing. John made it clear that he (John) was not the Savior, only a messenger who came to prepare the way for Christ. John's response was summed up in verse 30: "He must increase, but I must decrease."

John impressed upon his disciples that if they believed in God they would have eternal life. He says in verse 33, "Whoever receives his testimony sets his seal to this, that God is true." And in verse 36, "Whoever believes in the Son has eternal life." To reject God, or Jesus His Son, would result in spiritual death. He couldn't have stated this more powerfully. Through baptism, both Jesus and John were inviting people into a deeper relationship with God and offering them the opportunity to express joyful celebration that their lives were now committed to Christ.

Simply stated, belief in Jesus offers the gift of life. Rejection of Jesus results in spiritual death (v. 36). Thanks to God, He has provided a way for us to approach His throne. He has sent His Son to bridge the gap from us to God. When Jesus died, the ultimate sacrifice was made and will forever cover us in grace if we simply believe in Him. The message of Jesus is pure. The invitation is waiting—we need only accept. If we do accept, baptism is a way to announce that we are children of God. It's an expression that we have changed within. No longer defined by our sin, we have been washed by His blood and made clean. God invites us to accept His Son Jesus and to begin living a *new* life with Him. Our new life begins on the day we place our trust in Him and continues every day after that.

Promise

Therefore, if anyone is in Christ, he is a new creation. The old has passed away; behold, the new has come. (2 Corinthians 5:17)

John 3
New, Part 2

Something new. Most people regularly hope for something fresh and new in life. I think of words like *breakthrough* or *epiphany*. Nothing compares to a personal touch from God. If you have experienced this, then you know what we are talking about! Jesus brings life in a new way not only on the day of our initial salvation but also every day after that. Living in a broken world full of darkness often brings moments of despair. As you remember Jesus explaining the term "born again" to Nicodemus, may you remember that God offers new life to you. He offers a way to turn despair into hope. You never know, a touch of new life and light might be just around the corner. Keep seeking Jesus and you will find Him.

Process
1. Recite John 3:16 replacing "the world" and "whosoever" with your name.
2. On a scale of 1 to 10, how alive does your soul feel today?
3. If you have been baptized, think back to that time. Did you fully understand the implications? If not, or if you were too young to remember, consider a recommitment to Him, acknowledging that this washing with water represents the washing of your soul by God.
4. Is there a specific sin that weighs you down and prohibits you from believing that you are truly clean before God?
5. If repentance is simply reconnecting with God, consider what that might mean for you at this moment.

Prayer

God, You promised to make all things new. I come to You today and ask You to give me a fresh touch for which I long. Help me to learn from Your tender hand how to live the life that You've offered to me as one who has been washed with Jesus's blood. Help me to recognize the lies of unbelief that fill me. Thank You for awakening my soul on the day I entered into a relationship with You. Thank You for what lies ahead, as I experience You anew every day.

Promises

And I will give you a new heart, and a new spirit I will put within you. And I will remove the heart of stone from your flesh and give you a heart of flesh. (Ezekiel 36:26)

Create in me a clean heart, O God,
    and renew a right spirit within me. (Psalm 51:10)

And he who was seated on the throne said, "Behold, I am making all things new." Also he said, "Write this down, for these words are trustworthy and true." (Revelation 21:5)

I will give them one heart and one way, that they may fear me forever, for their own good and the good of their children after them. (Jeremiah 32:39)

John 4
Known, Part 1

Jesus answered her, "If you knew the gift of God, and who it is that is saying to you, 'Give me a drink,' you would have asked him, and he would have given you living water."

—John 4:10

My mother is an avid bird watcher. Growing up, we always found bird books on our kitchen table alongside a pair of binoculars. Just the other day she texted me, "Be watching for the cedar waxwings that migrate through our area in the springtime." Sure enough, within a few days, the trees' branches outside my house were filled with tiny, chirping birds. When I was younger I didn't always value bird watching, but over time, I've grown to appreciate my mother's appreciation for birds. I've learned that, surprisingly, they can actually teach us a number of profound spiritual truths.

For my birthday this year, my parents gave me a new bird feeder and some special bird seed they jokingly call "sirloin bird food." Only the most committed of birdwatchers would spend this much money to feed the birds. When I went to hang the new feeder, I took the old one down and placed it on a nearby patio table. I filled the new feeder with the premium bird seed, then went inside, leaving the old one outside. A few hours later, I glanced outside expecting to see my happy birds feasting on the new, special food. But wait! I laughed out loud, and almost couldn't believe my eyes. There were no birds feasting from the new bird feeder. Instead, they were all gathered around the old bird feeder nibbling at the low-budget bird seed! *Those crazy birds*, I thought, knowing they had no idea they were missing out on a special treat. Of course, it didn't take them long to correct their mistake, and soon they were enjoying the new, delicious food.

John dedicates forty-seven verses to one single narrative in chapter 4. No other story is given as much time and focus in the book of John as the story we find here. Let's peer into this chapter with curiosity and discover its significance. The themes we find within might contain some of the most important messages Jesus brought to the people. What's the theme? Let's look and see.

John continues to teach deep truths by showing us Jesus's interactions with those around Him and how He treated people during His time on earth. We can be assured Jesus relates to us today much like He related to these Bible characters so many years ago. The scene opens in Sychar of Samaria, through which we find Jesus passing on His way to Galilee. Historically, "the Jews have no dealings with the Samaritans" (v. 9). We are not told why Jesus, as a Jew, stopped in Samaria when He could have passed straight through. Possibly, He saw the Samaritans as people who needed His love as much as anyone else; or maybe He knew about a certain conversation with a certain woman in which He was meant to engage. But for whatever reason, maybe both, He stopped in Samaria at Jacob's well—Jacob from the book of Genesis—around noon. This begins the story known as "The Woman at the Well."

As we listen in, we hear a conversation between Jesus and the Samaritan woman who had come to draw water at this well. At first, Jesus's words seemed judgmental and shaming to the woman, but then His words turned to love and grace. Jesus asked the Samaritan woman for a drink of water. Curious as to why a Jewish man would ask her for a drink, she questioned Him. Maybe she knew He would be judged by onlookers for this inter-action. In those times, history tells us, women typically drew water either early in the morning or late in the day, but here, the Bible tells us, she was drawing water at noon. Maybe she had a bad reputation and was trying to avoid the judgmental looks and whispers of others. Or maybe she was truly an outcast of society.

Nevertheless, when Jesus asked her to draw Him a drink of water, a conversation ensued. The two began to talk about a "liv-ing water" (v. 10) that He alone could offer her in return. She responded openly and honestly with questions about Him and His request. "How is it that you, a Jew, ask for a drink from me, a woman of Samaria?" (v. 9). "Where do you get that living water?" (v. 11). "Are you greater than our father Jacob? He gave us the well" (v. 12). It seems, for so many reasons, Jesus caught her atten-tion and stirred her curiosity. Her questions were quite direct, and Jesus's answers were direct as well. He turned the conver-sation from the need for physical water and its ability to quench thirst to the need for spiritual water that satisfies in a different way. "Jesus answered her, 'If you knew the gift of God, and who it is that is saying to you, "Give me a drink," you would have asked him, and he would have given you living water'" (John 4:10).

Jesus then acknowledged that He knew she had been married five times and was not married to the man with whom she was currently living (v. 18). She seemed to be surprised that Jesus knew the truth about her. She later said to the townspeople, "He told me all that I ever did" (v. 39). When she pointed out that they were standing on the place her fathers had worshipped, Jesus stressed to her the true importance of worship. "But the hour is coming, and is now here, when the true worshipers will worship the Father in spirit and truth, for the Father is seeking such people to worship him. God is spirit, and those who worship him must worship in spirit and truth" (vv. 23–24). The woman proceeded to tell Jesus that she believed the Messiah was coming. When He explained to her that He was the Messiah, she left her water jar at the well and excitedly went to tell the people about Him. "Can this be the Christ?" (v. 29). Because of the woman's story, and in spite of her reputation, the people headed to the well to find out more.

What do we see in this narrative about Jesus and the woman for whom He had compassion? He drew her in with conversation involving a parallel between physical and spiritual water. He didn't simply acknowledge her physical thirst, but He assured her that He could quench her deepest longings and spiritual thirsts. He knew what she needed, and He offered an answer to that need in the form of a relationship with God. His spirit of grace—or unmerited favor—spilled onto her. He lovingly accepted and welcomed her despite her choices. He didn't address her sin; He addressed something far more important. That something was salvation. And He told her that only He could offer the salvation for which she deeply thirsted.

The story of this everyday person, who might be similar to you or me, is a warm invitation to us from God. We are fully *known* by Him, just as we are fully loved by Him in spite of our failings. He is repurposing our stories and providing a new way forward with Him, if we will only believe in the One who cares for us. He does not judge or condemn us. He simply loves us.

Just like the birds, we have been offered the most satisfying nourishment. Let us accept what is right in front of us. Let us move away from the ordinary and accept the extraordinary gift of life provided by our Messiah, our Jesus. If we do, we have the opportunity to daily experience a satisfaction beyond imagination.

Promise

Remember these things, O Jacob,
   and Israel, for you are my servant;
I formed you; you are my servant;
   O Israel, you will not be forgotten by me. (Isaiah 44:21)

John 4
Known, Part 2

After taking a long look at the fourth chapter of John, we see that the narrative holds significant truths regularly taught by Jesus. Much time is spent talking about one woman—the woman at the well—who had, like we have, the opportunity to find significant life change. Jesus meets us at our deepest places of need. Let's look inward, focusing on our own lives and identifying our own needs. May God open our eyes to the revelations He gives us, and may we seek to only live in close relationship with Him. With curiosity, may we find the sweetness of God's grace as we return to Him, time and again, to find the security and significance for which we long and were made.

Process
1. What would be your well—your deepest places of need today?
2. Picture God drawing near to you because He promises to be with you.
3. Take time to look at Jesus's response to the woman. Believe that this is the way He responds to you as well.
4. What emotions do you think Jesus had for the woman? Do you believe He has these emotions for you as well?
5. Consider how much He loved you as He hung on the cross, saving you, providing a way for you to directly approach God. Feel an overwhelming thankfulness.

Prayer

God, I'm just an everyday person like the woman at the well, who finds it hard to believe that You, the Almighty, are interested in having a conversation with me. Thank You for the warm invitation that You have given me to lay my burdens at Your feet. I'm so grateful that while You fully know me, You still love me. Thank You for redeeming my story and my heart. Please guide me as I aim to walk more closely with You, and help me to believe that You unconditionally care for me. Thank You for loving me enough to give Your life on the cross.

Promises

Know that the LORD, he is God!
    It is he who made us, and we are his;
    we are his people, and the sheep of his pasture. (Psalm 100:3)

And they sang a new song, saying,
    "Worthy are you to take the scroll
    and to open its seals,
    for you were slain, and by your blood you ransomed people for
      God
    from every tribe and language and people and nation."
(Revelation 5:9)

For we are his workmanship, created in Christ Jesus for good works, which God prepared beforehand, that we should walk in them. (Ephesians 2:10)

John 5
Precious, Part 1

I have come in my Father's name.

—John 5:43

A beautiful, graceful, Chinese-American girl named Noa lives in my neighborhood. She is ten years old. Over the years, I've been fortunate to have become friends with Noa and her family. I will always think of her as the little "starfish girl," based on the English name of the orphanage from which she came. Some families choose to keep their adoption story quiet. Others, like Noa's, choose to share their story. Either way, adoption always stirs tender hearts. The unfolding of adoption paths prepared by God are nothing short of supernatural.

Hearing what they identified as a little girl's cry from somewhere in China, Noa's mom and dad pursued an international adoption. After realizing that adopting a healthy Chinese baby girl could take up to ten years, they made the difficult, but hopeful decision to bring a special needs baby home to live with them. The decision made, they eagerly anticipated the arrival of the newest member of their family! This path to adopting a baby with special needs was a much shorter one, and they received a call within a few weeks. "We have a baby girl who is hearing impaired that is ready for a home immediately. Will you take her?" This simple conversation held many implications. After several days and many, many prayers, it was agreed that little Noa would soon be welcomed into her new American family. Pictures of Noa helped her future family begin to fall in love with their brown-eyed girl. Malnutrition and hearing impairment only multiplied the compassion they already felt for their new daughter. Prayerfully, as Noa's new parents brought her home, they consulted with medical professionals to determine the best ways to care for her. They needed a plan to help her gain physical strength as well as determine the cause of her hearing loss. But most of all, she simply needed the unconditional love that comes from being part of a family.

At this point, the story of Noa took a surprising and wonderful turn. Shortly after adoption proceedings were finalized, Noa's parents began to address her physical issues. The doctor looked into her ears, and much to everyone's surprise, the explanation for her hearing loss was simple: a buildup of fluid had caused her inability to hear. Noa did not have a hearing impairment after all, and in fact, she was soon hearing sounds clearly. Her family realized that this was all part of God's plan to make sure they received their new baby as quickly as possible. This precious starfish girl was meant to be a part of their family, and God had paved the way.

Jesus frequently explained that His identity was found in His Father. We read many times throughout the New Testament where Jesus stated that He was not just connected to God, but as His Son, He was actually an extension of God (v. 19). In John 5, Jesus identified as God's Son. But what exactly does this mean? What does it mean that Jesus identified with His Father?

Identity is a hot topic these days. To identify with someone means to feel that you are similar to and can understand them or their situation. It means being closely associated and sharing strong likeness with them. With a better understanding of Jesus's identity as the Son of God, we will likewise begin to identify as children of God.

Let's look at how Jesus states His identity as the Son of God in John 5:

- "But Jesus answered them, 'My Father is working until now, and I am working.'" (v. 17)
- "So Jesus said to them, 'Truly, truly, I say to you, the Son can do nothing of his own accord, but only what he sees the Father doing. For whatever the Father does, that the Son does likewise. For the Father loves the Son and shows him all that he himself is doing.'" (vv. 19–20)
- "For as the Father has life in himself, so he has granted the Son also to have life in himself." (v. 26)
- "I can do nothing on my own. As I hear, I judge, and my judgment is just, because I seek not my own will but the will of him who sent me." (v. 30)
- "For the works that the Father has given me to accomplish, the very works that I am doing, bear witness about me that the Father has sent me. And the Father who sent me has himself borne witness about me. His voice you have never heard, his form you have never seen." (vv. 36–37)
- "I have come in my Father's name." (v. 43)

It almost seems redundant as Jesus continues to make His point about identity, one He clearly doesn't want us to miss. A simple way of thinking about this is to consider genetics. Family resemblance refers to a similarity in the way people look because they are related to one another. But when looking at someone's identity in God, we aren't looking at an outward resemblance, but rather an inward one. When you believe and live as a child of

God, your soul identifies with Him and bears His image, or His resemblance.

Let's consider the verses mentioned above and our identity with God as our Father. It's astonishing to think that because of God's grace we have this privilege. As we continue to move through the book of John, we will understand the opportunity to claim a new identity in Jesus, a new life in Christ. Because of the sacrifice Jesus made on the cross, we can adopt His perfect record of righteousness and reunite with God the Father. As a result, the Bible tells us that we are precious to Him because of what He has done for us. First John 3:1 says, "See what kind of love the Father has given to us, that we should be called children of God; and so we are." The thought of this is both overwhelming and endearing.

Like Noa, we need a Father who loves us unconditionally and receives us into His forever family. Apart from God, we are unfulfilled and incomplete. We all have a desire to belong, and when we don't, our identity can be shaken. We feel weak and insecure. We need forgiveness. We need healing, and most of all, we need love. His heart goes out to us when He finds us sick and broken. He welcomes us into His family, and our identity is changed. We are made new and whole. He receives us as His own, and we are transformed. We emerge in a new way, realizing that we are healed. He sees our beauty and grace. We belong to a new family. Living within this bond of love provides a security and freedom that nothing on this earth can offer.

We meet in the yard for pleasant conversation. The twinkle in Noa's eyes and the way she leans into her mom reveal so much about her identity. She lives within a new bond of love. She belongs to a new family. What a beautiful parallel to Jesus's offer of love for us. Those who believe are welcomed into the family of

God. *Precious* in His sight, we have the opportunity to belong to Him. And that is more than enough.

Promise

Because you are precious in my eyes and honored, and I love you. (Isaiah 43:4)

John 5
Precious, Part 2

The analogy of adoption is used a number of times in God's Word. It's such a beautiful picture of a deep and personal relationship with God, our Father. When you picture yourself as the adopted child, you can begin to understand how your new identity comes from your adoptive Father. One's identity is deeply rooted in the family to whom he or she belongs. Imagine all of the gifts and benefits that come from being part of a royal family. These benefits are offered to you because you are chosen, handpicked by God, to be a part of His grand family. As you believe, you will receive a sense of security and acceptance that is unconditional, complete, and lasts forever.

Process
1. How would you define what it means to be adopted as a child of God?
2. Do you see yourself as bearing your heavenly Father's name?
3. If you did see yourself as part of God's family, how would this change the way you see yourself?
4. What lies creep into your head and cause you to disconnect from this relationship that God has made available to you?
5. Open your ears to hear your Father's voice saying, "You are precious to Me."

Prayer

Father, I desperately need unconditional love. I know that if I believe, You will receive me into Your forever family. Apart from You, I am unfulfilled and incomplete. I want to belong and be accepted. I need an identity that cannot be shaken. So often I feel weak and insecure. I need forgiveness. Thank You that Your heart goes out to me because You love me. Thank You for the opportunity to emerge in a new way, realizing that You not only created me, but You also welcome me as Your child. Help me to live within this bond of love and find the freedom You offer as a result.

Promises

You have led in your steadfast love the people whom you have
    redeemed;
  you have guided them by your strength to your holy abode.
(Exodus 15:13)

And they shall be called The Holy People,
  The Redeemed of the LORD;
and you shall be called Sought Out,
  A City Not Forsaken. (Isaiah 62:12)

Listen to me, O coastlands,
  and give attention, you peoples from afar.
The LORD called me from the womb,
  from the body of my mother he named my name. (Isaiah 49:1)

John 6
Nourished, Part 1

Jesus said to them, "I am the bread of life; whoever comes to me shall not hunger, and whoever believes in me shall never thirst."

—John 6:35

As we continue to discover truths in the book of John, it's not surprising that chapter 5, with its theme of dissatisfaction and longing, is followed by chapter 6, with its theme of satisfaction and fulfillment. This sixth chapter—the longest chapter in the Gospel of John with seventy-one verses—delivers a rich feast of spiritual truth.

Not long ago in the Deep South, we Alabamians experienced something unexpected. A cold front moved in one winter and along with it came frigid temperatures. Our mayor opened a local auditorium as a warming station for those who did not have access to heat. The manager of the auditorium posted on social media that the folks sheltering there during the bitter cold weather would need food, water, blankets, coats, etc. My neighbor shared this information with me, and we decided to try and help. We put our heads together and came up with an idea: sandwiches! That was it! We would enlist the help of our friends and make sandwiches for the people staying in the warming station. Within a few hours, we came up with a detailed plan: we would immediately text as many people as possible who we thought might be willing to help. We would ask them to make ten sand-wiches apiece and drop them off at my doorstep, and then we'd deliver the sandwiches to the auditorium. Over the next few days, I continued to find boxes and bags filled with sandwiches at my house. Our goal was two hundred sandwiches, but fifteen hundred sandwiches later, we had to send out a message to the sand-wich-making army: "Thank you, but we have more than enough!" This simple idea provided food for many, many people.

It was a joyful experience, as you might imagine, watching God's people eagerly step up to help those in need. But John 6 opens with a problem that could only be solved by Jesus. We find the masses of curious and spiritually needy people once again fol-lowing Jesus and His disciples. "And a large crowd was following him, because they saw the signs that he was doing on the sick" (v. 2). When Jesus realized that the thousands of people—roughly five thousand (v. 10)—needed food, He looked to the disciples. He asked Philip if he knew of a place to buy bread for the crowd. The disciples must have been alarmed as they discussed how much it would cost to feed so many people. But Jesus knew where this con-versation was headed, and surely, He was excited about what He was preparing to do. Andrew pointed out that the only food avail-able was in the hands of a small boy who had brought along a meal of five loaves of bread and two fish. "Have the people sit down," Jesus said (v. 10). The disciples might have been shaking their heads or rolling their eyes, but they did what Jesus instructed, and five thousand people sat down. "Jesus then took the loaves, and when he had given thanks, he distributed them to those who were seated. So also the fish, as much as they wanted. And when they had eaten their fill, he told his disciples, 'Gather up the leftover fragments, that nothing may be lost'" (vv. 11–12). We can only imagine what it must have been like that day on the grassy hill-side. The crowd of hungry people had been miraculously provided a satisfying meal. Many must have immediately believed that Jesus was indeed the Son of God. Time and time again, we see Jesus performing miracles that have profound implications. Jesus had not only provided for the physical needs of the people that day, but He also had *nourished* their souls.

After Jesus miraculously fed five thousand people with one lit-tle boy's lunch, He goes on, in chapter 6, to perform yet another surprising miracle. Skeptics have tried to dismiss this next mir-acle, this phenomenon of Jesus walking on water, with scientific explanations. But something tells me that if they had been in the boat that day, they too would have believed that Jesus was the Son of God. "When [the disciples] had rowed about three or four miles, they saw Jesus walking on the sea and coming near the boat, and they were frightened. But he said to them, 'It is I; do not be afraid'" (vv. 19–20). With every miracle Jesus performed, He provided building blocks for their faith. He seemed to serve them evidence of His divinity on a silver platter as He performed mira-cles right in front of their eyes. "Jesus answered them, 'This is the work of God, that you believe in him whom he has sent'" (v. 29).

The following day Jesus circles back to the theme of nour-ishment. With the miracle of feeding five thousand people still fresh on the minds of His disciples, Jesus began a conversation about how He was the bread of life. In verses 32–35, He clearly laid out the concept of spiritual nourishment when He said, "'But my Father gives you the true bread from heaven. For the bread of God is he who comes down from heaven and gives life to the world.' They said to him, 'Sir, give us this bread always.' Jesus said to them, 'I am the bread of life; whoever comes to me shall not hunger, and whoever believes in me shall never thirst.'"

Jesus takes the theme of spiritual nourishment further still when He gives first mention of what is known as the sacrament of communion. Communion is the service of Christian worship at which bread and wine are administered as a symbolic act of receiving the presence of Christ. "This is the bread that comes down from heaven, so that one may eat of it and not die. I am the living bread that came down from heaven. If anyone eats of this bread, he will live forever. And the bread that I will give for the life of the world is my flesh" (vv. 50–51). He beautifully and creatively invited them, as He invites us, to experience His presence. When we feast on His words and His nourishment, they are rich and satisfying.

As some turned away, Jesus asked if any of His twelve disciples also felt led to leave (vv. 66–67). Peter responds almost desperately, "Lord, to whom shall we go? You have the words of eternal life" (v. 68). Peter knew and acknowledged that Jesus was the Holy One of God. To him, staying with Jesus was a no-brainer. He couldn't imagine not continuing the journey with His Lord. Can you relate to Peter? Do you know in whom true nourishment is found? If you've never experienced this spiritual nourishment, why not sample what He has to offer by placing your trust in Him? Follow alongside Him, and you will begin to experience life in a new way and with new purpose.

Jesus offers a rich feast for our souls. He provides for His children in amazing ways, sometimes through fellow believers. He can turn five loaves and two fish into a feast for five thousand or two hundred sandwiches into fifteen hundred on a frigid day in Alabama. Jesus cared for the people when He was on earth, and

He cares for us now. Are you hungry for more? Believe in Him, and you will receive the satisfying nourishment for which you are longing.

Promise
And my God will supply every need of yours according to his riches in glory in Christ Jesus. (Philippians 4:19)

John 6
Nourished, Part 2

A strong theme in John 6 is one of trust. At times there are overwhelming obstacles and challenges before us, and we do not feel strong or capable enough to handle these difficulties in life. Trusting God provides the ability to feel complete in areas where you often feel lacking. Can you trust Him to feed your soul when you are spiritually hungry? Can you take one step at a time, walking by faith, as you hear His call? Can you fully believe He is going to care for you and that nothing is out of His control? He is a God who can be trusted, and you can be sure that He is a God who provides for you more completely than you can possibly imagine.

Process

1. Where on earth do you tend to look for satisfaction and fulfillment?
2. Pause for a minute and prayerfully acknowledge your spiritual neediness.
3. Can you remember a time that you received miraculous provision? Consider God's faithfulness in that moment.
4. How might you make a new commitment to regularly recognize your hunger and turn to God for nourishment?
5. Is God calling you to trust Him in order to "walk on water" at this moment? Ask Him to help you place your trust in Him as you take the first step.

Prayer

Jesus, may I take a seat at the table and feast with You today. When I realize that You offer rich nourishment for my soul, I am able to acknowledge my insatiable hunger. I long for You. I long to be filled with Your spiritual provision. Thank You for providing for me. Give me the strength to depend on You when circumstances arise that I am unable to handle. I know that You care for me and You will always understand my deepest needs better than I understand them myself. Help me put my trust in You and in turn receive the satisfying nourishment that only comes from You.

Promises

The LORD is my shepherd; I shall not want. (Psalm 23:1)

And God is able to make all grace abound to you, so that having all sufficiency in all things at all times, you may abound in every good work. (2 Corinthians 9:8)

Trust in the LORD with all your heart,
    and do not lean on your own understanding.
In all your ways acknowledge him,
    and he will make straight your paths. (Proverbs 3:5–6)

John 7
Validated, Part 1

*If anyone thirsts, let him come to me and drink. Who-
ever believes in me, as the Scripture has said, "Out of
his heart will flow rivers of living water."*

—John 7:37–38

Not long ago, I watched a show about Richard Jewell. For those
who remember Jewell, some think he was a hero, some a villain.
Richard Jewell, a security guard at the 1996 Olympic Games in
Atlanta, GA, discovered a backpack containing three pipe bombs
on the park grounds. Just before the bombs detonated, he notified
the police and warned people to quickly evacuate the area. It's been
said that his heroic act saved approximately one hundred lives.
But shortly after the bombing, the FBI—and the media—quickly
found someone to blame. That someone was Richard Jewell. A
story was concocted, and Jewell became a person of interest—his
face plastered across the news, his name in the headlines. Anxious
minds eased, and the Olympic Games continued with news that
the bomber had been identified. But five years later, Eric Rudolph,
the real Olympic Park bomber was found, and evidence, along
with a confession, proved Rudolph's guilt. After years of enduring
false accusations, Richard Jewell was exonerated.

John 7 tells us a story about the life of Jesus when dissenting
opinions about Him began to arise. With every passing day, the
Jewish leaders felt more threatened by Him. People became con-

fused and doubts arose. They had so longed for hope from a savior, but the religious leaders of the day, along with their followers, were skeptical that Jesus was who He claimed to be (v. 12). They even sought to kill Him (v. 1). His message seemed contrary to their beliefs and the lives they had built around religious rules and performance. Accusations flew and rumors soared about Jesus. The people suddenly had to decide, "Do I believe this man, or do I side with the leaders I've always trusted and followed?" The people grew conflicted. Was this man the promised Messiah for whom they had hoped, or was He a false prophet to be dismissed or even worse? They "muttered" and "marveled" in the very same breath (vv. 12, 15).

Jesus responded to the lies and unbelief by explaining His relationship to God. "My teaching is not mine, but his who sent me" (v. 16). "The one who speaks on his own authority seeks his own glory; but the one who seeks the glory of him who sent him is true, and in him there is no falsehood" (v. 18). He presented His case by reminding them of their trusted forefather, Moses, in whose words and prophecies they believed. He continued to challenge their accusations by calling them to seek the truth. "You know me, and you know where I come from. But I have not come of my own accord. He who sent me is true, and him you do not know" (v. 28).

As the conversations continued, we can only imagine how Jesus must have felt. He knew He was God's Son, the Savior, but the people did not. They began taking sides. It must have been incredibly difficult to hear their slandering words. He was innocent, but many labeled Him a liar. He had a choice: to listen to the accusations or to live according to God's plan for Him. From agreement and conviction to confusion and controversy—this would define Jesus's life until the time of His death.

So what does this story have to do with us? Each day we struggle to fight lies coming from our culture as well as from the voices in our heads. "You are not who God says you are." "You are a fake." "You have no purpose here." "How dare you claim to be a child of God. Just look at your thoughts and behavior!" The list of internal accusations never ends. We, like Jesus, must live in the truth of who God says we are regardless of how we might feel about ourselves.

What did Jesus do when surrounded by and confronted with the people's doubts? How did He deal with these accusations? The answer lies in the words "believed" and "receive" (v. 39). In fact, Jesus was very emotional about His desire for the people to realize that He truly belonged to God, His Father, and was sent to earth by Him. Verse 37 tells us Jesus "cried out." He urged them with a great plea to believe and said, "If anyone thirsts, let him come to me and drink. Whoever believes in me, as the Scripture has said, 'Out of his heart will flow rivers of living water'" (vv. 37–38).

This truth, this promise overcomes the lies that sometimes consume our thoughts. Even if the voices of doubt come, they don't have to define us or bring shame. There is always a plethora of evidence to convict us when we examine our sinful lives. We feel like frauds when we see ourselves apart from Jesus. We're only *validated* when defined by His perfect record rather than our imperfect one. Praise God, we can claim Jesus's righteousness, and no person or thought can argue against it! We only need to believe that God is our Father and we will receive the new identity that validates us as His son or daughter. This validation comes on the day we place our belief and trust in Jesus and remains for the rest of our lives.

The story in chapter 7 closes with Nicodemus, Jesus's friend and a new believer, arguing with the people. "Nicodemus, who had gone to him before, and who was one of them, said to them, 'Does our law judge a man without first giving him a hearing and learning what he does?'" (vv. 50–51). In attempting to convince them to believe, he is saying, "Just try it out. Give belief in Jesus a chance. Take a risk and see if it makes sense!"

Imagine the feeling Richard Jewell had the day he was finally exonerated. The relief and freedom must have been overwhelming. As you allow the truth of God to become the authority in your life and to penetrate your soul, you too will come to know a joy and freedom that cannot be matched. In Christ you are no longer guilty, and in fact, your record has been wiped completely and perfectly clean.

Promise
And be found in him, not having a righteousness of my own that comes from the law, but that which comes through faith in Christ, the righteousness from God that depends on faith. (Philippians 3:9)

John 7
Validated, Part 2

Emotions intensified in John 7, and it's hard to understand how Jesus held up beneath the slander and accusations that were continuously hurled at Him during the time preceding His death. In our broken world full of conflict, we also sometimes face constant lies and accusations that can penetrate our souls and render us hopeless. And the lies within can prove even stronger, causing us to shut down. We see that Jesus handled these attacks by connecting with His Father, believing that God loved Him and had a specific purpose for everything that took place. We have this same opportunity to connect with Him, believing and trusting in God, no matter how we might feel.

Process
1. How have you allowed the messages of this world to dishearten you?
2. What are some of the lies or accusations in your head that are on repeat?
3. How must Jesus have felt when the people falsely accused Him?
4. Can you see that He relates to you when you feel alone?
5. How can you, like Jesus, align with your new identity and live according to God's plan?

Prayer

God, I want to believe that what You say about me is true. I know that because of Your Son's death on the cross, You value me. You don't hold things against me. Thank You that His perfect record has replaced my imperfect one. Your grace overwhelms me. Please allow Your voice to fill me when I doubt myself and have feelings of inadequacy and insecurity. Please penetrate my soul with confidence in Your Holy Spirit. Because of Jesus, help me to live free from guilt. Thank You for making me clean on the day of my salvation as well as today and every day going forward.

Promises

In those days Judah will be saved, and Jerusalem will dwell securely. And this is the name by which it will be called: "The LORD is our Righteousness." (Jeremiah 33:16)

For in it the righteousness of God is revealed from faith for faith, as it is written, "The righteous shall live by faith." (Romans 1:17)

And because of him you are in Christ Jesus, who became to us wisdom from God, righteousness and sanctification and redemption. (1 Corinthians 1:30)

John 8
Accepted, Part 1

And Jesus said, "Neither do I condemn you; go, and from now on sin no more."

—John 8:11

Over time and throughout history, the people of our country have expressed strong opinions. From moral division to political division, most seem to have different, and usually strong, opinions. But in recent years, since the birth of social media, we have crossed into new territory with the way we express these opinions. It has become commonplace to convey one's ideas on public forums, unfiltered, with disrespect or even hate. We've created a virtual stockade, a new method of public shaming. Many believe that their opinions are truth and, with confidence and arrogance, shame others who are different. Public shaming, formerly known as judging, is now referred to as "canceling."

So how did we get here? When did it become acceptable to embarrass people, ruin their reputation, boycott their business, or in extreme cases, ruin their life just because we disagree? And if we believe in our heart and soul that others are wrong, should it be our responsibility to judge or cancel them? Ironically, John chapter 8 speaks directly to this modern-day issue. In fact, Jesus Himself addressed it. Thankfully, we can look into the Gospel of John and find out not only what Jesus said about public shaming but also look at what He did.

Chapter 8 begins with Jesus teaching in the temple. We're told the scribes and Pharisees—those who interpreted the religious laws and those who enforced them—brought a woman deemed a sinner before Him. "Teacher," they said, "this woman has been caught in the act of adultery. Now in the Law, Moses commanded us to stone such women. So what do you say?" (vv. 4–5). The religious leaders, threatened by Jesus's growing influence, were attempting to test Him, to put Him in a lose-lose situation with His back against the wall. He would be forced to either agree with the laws of Moses and condemn this woman to death or refuse to condemn her, contradicting their religious law. So what did Jesus do? Did He publicly shame this woman? The answer is no. He absolutely did not judge, shame, or cancel her. Instead, He did a beautiful, bold, loving thing. He showed her grace; He showed her favor she did not deserve. And ultimately, He showed her love.

As the religious leaders continued to press Jesus for an answer, He stood up. "Let him who is without sin among you be the first to throw a stone at her" (v. 7). He had called their bluff. He had turned the tables on them and, by asking a simple question, forced them to consider their own sin rather than hers. When they heard His challenge, we're told they went away one by one until Jesus was left alone with the woman. What irony! The angry, judgmental leaders slinking away speechless, and the woman left standing with Jesus, unconditionally accepted by Him. The sinner condemned to death found herself safely standing before her Savior. He asked her, " 'Has no one condemned you?' She said, 'No one, Lord.' And Jesus said, 'Neither do I condemn you; go, and from now on sin no more' " (vv. 10–11).

This profound statement in verse 11 displays the grace Jesus poured out on this woman. Sometimes, we as believers tend to practice "sin management." If I do _____, I'll compensate for my sin. Go to church. Read my Bible. Confess my sins. Change my behavior. Study a Christian book. Attend therapy. While this list of to-dos may be a part of the Christian faith, clearly there is a different picture before us in this story. Within this narrative lies the secret of true freedom. Let's look at the woman's response. The grace Jesus poured over her broken heart surely motivated her to do exactly as He commanded. We've all, at one time, received grace from someone. It's most humbling when you know you're wrong and someone doesn't hold it against you. Maybe a teacher let you pass a test you should have failed, or a police officer gave you a warning rather than a ticket. That feeling of relief and gratitude fuels us to do better in the future.

In fact, this motivation to "sin no more" is deeply rooted in a relationship with Jesus, not a list of rules. While spiritual good works can be beautiful expressions of gratitude and worship, they can never be the way to freedom. Instead, God's grace, showered over and through our lives, drives us to run from sin. Want to sin less? Seek a greater understanding of God and the grace He offers us. When grace has its effect on a soul, the result is inexpressible gratitude, which results in obedience. I would love to have spoken with the woman that day. I would love to have seen the look in her eyes. I'm sure her expression would have been tender and humble. Jesus's grace for us was manifested on the cross. Because we were full of sin and brokenness, He died on the cross for us. We did not do anything to deserve or earn His grace. Grace means He did everything; we did nothing. Our chains of guilt have been cut. We've been given a clean record going forward. It sounds too good to be true.

Condemnation can lock chains around your soul. The voices of the enemy whisper, "Who do you think you are? You aren't good enough! Shame on you. Try harder." While the fact that we aren't good enough is true, the voice of shame is a lie. Because our worth is based on Jesus's record rather than our own, we are deemed worthy. "Worthy is the Lamb who was slain, to receive power and wealth and wisdom and might and honor and glory and blessing!" (Rev. 5:12). Our sin and shame were swapped once and for all by Jesus's death on the cross. He took the punishment for the sins of the human race, and all who believe are set free. "So if the Son sets you free, you will be free indeed" (v. 36). Grace is the cornerstone of a relationship with Jesus: the beginning, the middle, and the end. Fueled by His grace, with gratitude, we have the privilege of living a life that honors Him.

We can only imagine how the woman felt as she stood before Jesus, accused of a sin that warranted death. One moment the woman faced death by stoning, the next she was free. What a beautiful picture of God's love for us. He knows we are full of sin and imperfection, but when He looks at us, He sees Jesus. He sees perfection. For this reason, despite our sin, we are *accepted* and free to go. We are not judged or canceled by Him. It is because of this grace that we will desire to please Him. Only through the power of God and the sacrifice of Jesus is our devotion to Him possible. And only because of His love.

Promise

There is therefore now no condemnation for those who are in Christ Jesus. (Romans 8:1)

John 8
Accepted, Part 2

Many of us may not have experienced outright public shaming like the woman in John 8. But because all of us have experienced shame at one time or another, the topic is quite relevant in the therapy world today. When internalized, shame can cut deep and determine how you view yourself. Consider that Jesus's words to this woman are also words that you might hear from Him today. The book of Hebrews says that Jesus despised the shame He felt on the cross (12:2). He has gone before us, experiencing shame on our behalf. There are no words to describe the deep love He showed for us by going through the darkness on our behalf.

Process
1. Think about a time currently or in the past that you have felt shame.
2. What emotions do you think the woman felt when the religious leaders criticized her?
3. What words did Jesus express to her that extended grace? Imagine Him saying those same words to you.
4. How do you think she felt when Jesus affirmed her?
5. How do you feel when you are able to receive Jesus's acceptance of you?

Prayer
God, I can only wonder how the woman felt that day as she stood before your Son Jesus. You offer me more forgiveness than I can

possibly imagine. I'm grateful for this picture of Your love. Thank You that although I am imperfect, when You look at me, You see Your perfect Son, Jesus, and despite my sin, I'm accepted and free to go. Your grace makes me want to live for You. Please remind me this Easter that I can only serve You through the power of Your Spirit, remembering that Jesus died on the cross for me.

Promises

And the free gift is not like the result of that one man's sin. For the judgment following one trespass brought condemnation, but the free gift following many trespasses brought justification. (Romans 5:16)

For the law of the Spirit of life has set you free in Christ Jesus from the law of sin and death. (Romans 8:2)

For all have sinned and fall short of the glory of God, and are justified by his grace as a gift, through the redemption that is in Christ Jesus. (Romans 3:23–24)

John 9
Anointed, Part 1

Though I was blind, now I see.

—John 9:25

Modern medicine—any new form of medical discovery or advancement—emerged in the eighteenth century after the Industrial Revolution. With the rapid growth of economic activity in Western Europe and America, there were amazing advancements. Brilliant minds came together with technology, providing significant progress in medicine. Scientific discoveries and inventions helped identify, prevent, and treat illnesses. With this better understanding of how the human body worked, people who lived with physical afflictions were no longer hopeless.

Some of us can't imagine how those suffering with ailments and diseases face their day-to-day emotional distress. When sick people are cured by medical advancements, it is thrilling. For example, it's moving to watch people with vision or hearing impairments receive treatment which enables them to see or hear like never before. Their faces light up and eyes widen when they first experience sight or sound. They come alive in a new way that is awe-inspiring to the rest of us. Can you imagine hearing someone's voice for the first time after living your entire life in complete silence? Picture someone seeing colorful images like a bright red rose or a deep blue sky that he or she has only ever heard of but never before experienced. Or how must people feel when they receive a new prosthesis and are able to walk for the first time? What about cancer patients who receive the news they've been cured? These medical miracles surely must be the most precious gifts a person could ever receive.

John 9 opens with the story of a man who had been born blind. The disciples asked Jesus whether this man's blindness resulted from his own sin or the sin of his parents. "Jesus answered, 'It was not that this man sinned, or his parents, but that the works of God might be displayed in him'" (v. 3). He was already beginning to turn the disciples' minds from the physical to the spiritual world. With empathy, Jesus approached the man. He did something unexpected, something that might be described as distasteful or even gross. Jesus spit on the ground and made mud with His saliva. He then touched the man's eyes with the mud He made, and after spreading this mud over the man's eyes, He told him to go wash in the pool of Siloam. The man did exactly what Jesus said—he went and washed—and he returned seeing. It's probably safe to assume that he also returned shocked and ecstatic and extremely grateful.

While it's not discussed in this ninth chapter of John, let's consider the irony of the mud. The temple held purified water with which worshippers would wash before entering. They were required to cleanse themselves in order to come before God. Other mediums were also used for purification and included oil for healing. Each medium held deep meaning, and most were used in a physical manner by the leaders. Additionally, the high priests and their descendants were anointed—or smeared or rubbed with oil—to mark them as holy and set apart to the Lord. On the day Jesus met the blind man, He did not use religious purification or healing mediums. Instead, He simply used dirt and spit. It seems He wanted to make a point. Jesus didn't need holy water or fine oil to heal the blind man. He only needed the power of God.

He seemed to illustrate that life with Him would be organic, or unfold naturally, rather than formulated and structured. Jesus knew that apart from Him, the people would never be pure. But He did not then, nor does He now, require purity. Instead, through His perfect record and life given for us, He has provided our path to God, a path filled with spiritual sight and understanding. Jesus covers His children's imperfections with His perfection, just like He covered the blind man's eyes with mud. And the result is that we are healed forever.

This one miracle is discussed three times in chapter 9 (vv. 6, 11, 15). Let's dig deeper and find out why. Time and again, we see that Jesus came to heal the people and offer them a relationship with God. But the religious leaders of the day offered only religious rules and regulations. Concerned that Jesus had broken their Sabbath rules, they couldn't even appreciate this astounding miracle. They continued to question the blind man, his parents, and also Jesus about what had happened, seeking to prove that He was not sent by God. They wanted to discredit His teaching, His miracles, and His authority. Why? Because while they offered strict laws, He poured out grace. They felt threatened by this man who had upended their entire belief system and way of life. They were so caught up in their traditions that they were blind to the power of God staring them in the face.

Jesus performed miracles not only to demonstrate His power but also, more importantly, to paint a picture of a spiritual life offered through a relationship with God. This entire chapter reveals a Savior who came to heal both physical and spiritual afflictions. He came to offer spiritual sight and life to those whose souls live in darkness.

The Lenten season precedes Easter. It begins on Ash Wednesday, a day of humble repentance. Many confess their sins in preparation for the coming celebration of Easter. The pastor or priest smears ash in the shape of a cross on the foreheads of believers. These repentance ashes mark the beginning of the Easter season. But what marks the end of the season? The torturous death followed by the glorious resurrection of Jesus, all on our behalf. Because life overcame death, we can see and experience this anointing, this beauty from ashes, this marking of our souls as holy and set apart to the Lord.

So how do we see ourselves? Do we see our ashes or His perfection? Do we recognize that as children of God, we are *anointed* by Him? We have been healed by His blood and our sight has been restored. As we come to trust in Him, He offers us the gift of a life that we would otherwise never know, a life of unimaginable joy. As He said in verse 39, "I came into this world, that those who do not see may see."

Promise

To grant to those who mourn in Zion—
    to give them a beautiful headdress instead of ashes,
the oil of gladness instead of mourning,
    the garment of praise instead of a faint spirit;
that they may be called oaks of righteousness,
    the planting of the LORD, that he may be glorified. (Isaiah 61:3)

John 9
Anointed, Part 2

In chapter 9, John narrates a story about a profound miracle that demonstrated Jesus's magnificent power. Not only was His power on display but also the gift of spiritual healing through a relationship with Him. Communion with God provides the salve that our soul needs to heal physical, mental, and spiritual afflictions. Because of Jesus's torturous death on the cross followed by His glorious resurrection, we, as His people, can live with His continual healing. On that first Easter morning, life overcame sin and death, allowing us to live in a new reality of hope and freedom.

Process
1. How do you see yourself today as someone who needs healing?
2. Do you see your sins' ashes covered by His perfection?
3. How do you feel when you recognize that you are a child of God, the great physician?
4. Is there someone you know who has found healing from God? Consider asking him or her about it.
5. Next time you celebrate communion, remember this is a time set aside for God to heal *you*.

Prayer
Jesus, as I see You during this Lenten season, I reflect back on the days that You walked this earth, spreading the acceptance of Your Father to people just like me. You've covered my unholiness

with Your holiness, just like You covered the blind man's eyes with mud. The result is that I am healed forever. Help my connection with You to be organic—to unfold naturally—as I get to know you better. Keep me from a religious, structured way of life that only leads to pride or discouragement. With Your help and grace, allow me to see myself as pure because of You. The journey to the cross brought deep sadness, but, thankfully, joy and celebration followed with the discovery of the empty tomb! For this I'm beyond grateful. Your perfect record and life given for me is too much to comprehend. Please allow me spiritual sight and understanding through Your anointing.

Promises

For the LORD takes pleasure in his people;
    he adorns the humble with salvation. (Psalm 149:4)

I bring near my righteousness; it is not far off,
    and my salvation will not delay;
I will put salvation in Zion,
    for Israel my glory. (Isaiah 46:13)

Your sun shall no more go down,
    nor your moon withdraw itself;
for the LORD will be your everlasting light,
    and your days of mourning shall be ended. (Isaiah 60:20)

John 10
Belonging, Part 1

*My sheep hear my voice, and I know them, and they
follow me. I give them eternal life, and they will never
perish, and no one will snatch them out of my hand.*
—John 10:27–28

Halfway into the book of John, we have become familiar with
Jesus's style of teaching. He effectively communicated with
carefully chosen words. His narratives touched His listeners by
not only drawing them in but also stirring their curiosity. They
wanted to understand the analogies as well as the man teaching them and, in so doing, to figure out if they could believe His
claim to be the promised Savior.

Not long ago, I was checking out in the grocery store line. I
heard a voice behind me speaking above the crowd. It was a voice
I would have recognized anywhere! Although I hadn't heard
this voice in many years, I would never have forgotten it. It was
the animated voice of a high school friend that I hadn't seen in
decades. I had no doubt it was her, and when I turned around,
sure enough, there she stood.

Voice recognition is intriguing. Our Creator could have made
all voices sound the same, but He didn't. Just like fingerprints and
faces, there are no two voices alike. Today, with the advancement
of technology, voice recognition has grown relevant in a new way.
Phones and smart speakers can learn our voices and respond to

us with music, the weather report, or the daily news. My speaker's owner's manual instructed me to give it a command. "Learn my voice," I began. After repeating three or four more statements, my speaker responded, "Thanks, I got it." Now, only I can talk to my speaker and get a response. No one else's voice will invoke a reply.

John 10 provides one of Jesus's most compelling narratives. He told a story about a shepherd and the deep love he had for his sheep. He led them into the pastures for feeding. He watched over them because they belonged to him. He protected them. Then Jesus went on to talk about a different caretaker. This keeper did not own the flock he tended, instead he was a hired hand. As a result, he did not care as deeply for his flock as the shepherd who owned his flock.

The disciples listened intently, but it must have been clear to Jesus that they did not understand His analogy. In a departure from the norm, He stated His point clearly, "I am the good shepherd. The good shepherd lays down his life for the sheep. He who is a hired hand and not a shepherd, who does not own the sheep, sees the wolf coming and leaves the sheep and flees, and the wolf snatches them and scatters them" (vv. 11–12). Jesus wanted them to understand that choosing to believe that He was the Son of God would mean they would belong to Him. This belief in Him would bring them into His fold of safety and care.

We also see an adversary in the story—a robber attempting to steal the flock. The sheep wouldn't follow the thief out of the pen because they didn't recognize his voice. They didn't trust him. But when the sheep recognized the voice of their shepherd, they willingly followed, knowing that he would care for them and protect them. "When he has brought out all his own, he goes before them, and the sheep follow him, for they know his voice" (v. 4).

The life that the good shepherd offers to those who follow him not only provides care and protection but also is described as bountiful. "The thief comes only to steal and kill and destroy. I came that they may have life and have it abundantly" (v. 10).

Next Jesus described the lengths to which the shepherd would go to protect his flock. The shepherd cared so deeply for his sheep that he would do anything to defend them. He would even stake his own life for the sake of the sheep that belonged to him. Jesus made this message personal when He revealed that as their Good Shepherd, this was also what He offered. "I lay down my life for the sheep" (v. 15). He gave His life for us, His sheep, when He died on the cross. He offers us His love, and along with it, a new life in Him. "My sheep hear my voice, and I know them, and they follow me. I give them eternal life, and they will never perish, and no one will snatch them out of my hand" (vv. 27–28).

If we believe in Him, we are offered a Good Shepherd that takes care of us. He desires to provide us an abundant life, one full of fulfillment and spiritual riches. Maybe it's time to turn up the volume. He is speaking. Do we hear Him? Do we recognize His voice? Or are we listening to a hired hand or an intruder? For believers, the adversary doesn't own us and will never care for us like the Good Shepherd. "I am the good shepherd. I know my own and my own know me" (v. 14). But when we belong to Him, we can cry out, and He promises to hear us. Concerned about our every need, He is always watching out for us.

Learn to recognize His voice. Become acquainted with it by spending time reading His Word and praying. Pour your heart out to Him and listen for His response. Repetition breeds familiarity and recognition. You are invited into a spiritually intimate relationship with Him. He is closer than you might imagine. He loves you because you are His. He gave up everything so that you can have everything, so that you can experience abundant life. Draw near and enter the fold of the One who loves you most.

Promise

To him the gatekeeper opens. The sheep hear his voice, and he calls his own sheep by name and leads them out. (John 10:3)

John 10
Belonging, Part 2

As we read the stories of Jesus and see how He personally related to those with whom He spent time on earth, we can't help but be drawn in with curiosity and wonder. Could it really be true that Jesus relates to us today in the very same way? On many occasions, the Bible uses the analogy of God, a Good Shepherd, and us, His sheep. Just like the sheep desperately need a tender, strong shepherd for provision and protection, we desperately need a tender and strong God. At Easter, we celebrate not only that He protects us and provides for us but also that Jesus ultimately laid down His life for us. This is the greatest sacrifice someone could make. Connecting with Him through His Word and in conversational prayer allows us to live with Him as our Good Shepherd, and as we do this, we will come to recognize His voice, just like the sheep learned how to recognize the voice of their shepherd.

Process
1. Do you feel close to God today? If not, when was the last time you felt His presence?
2. How has God protected you or provided for you over time?
3. How does it feel when God speaks to you in a special way?
4. If you have never experienced this closeness with Him, stop and ask Him to make His presence known in your life.
5. Who or what are the intruders that block your connection with God? Ask Him to protect you from them.

Prayer

Dear Father, thank You so much that You relate to me in an intimate way. Thank You that I can hear from You and experience Your loving-kindness through our relationship. Help me to recognize Your voice more clearly. Enable me to follow Your guidance. Protect me from evil that robs my relationship with You. Remind me that the devil does not own me. I belong to You, and when I cry out, You promise to hear me. You're concerned about my every need, and You're always watching out for me. Thank You that I can also come to recognize Your voice in my life. When I stay connected to You, I feel safe.

Promises

But if anyone loves God, he is known by God. (1 Corinthians 8:3)

But God's firm foundation stands, bearing this seal: "The Lord knows those who are his," and, "Let everyone who names the name of the Lord depart from iniquity." (2 Timothy 2:19)

He has redeemed my soul from going down into the pit,
    and my life shall look upon the light. (Job 33:28)

John 11
Alive, Part 1

Jesus said to her, "I am the resurrection and the life. Whoever believes in me, though he die, yet shall he live, and everyone who lives and believes in me shall never die."

—John 11:25–26

After Jesus shared the parable of the sheep in chapter 10, the crowds of Jewish people rose up against Him. Already, some had aggressively threatened to take His life by stoning (v. 8). But Jesus safely escaped the temple in Jerusalem, crossing the Jordan River to the place where John had baptized many believers. Teaching, healing, and touching the people spiritually, Jesus spent time in conversation with them, answering their questions and providing guidance and understanding. We're told many of these people came to believe in Him at this time. This is where the story we find in John 11 begins. It centers around a family Jesus loved. This family of three included Mary, who we will see in chapter 12 worshipfully anointing Jesus's feet with oil; her sister Martha, who we'll see working hard to prepare a beautiful meal for Jesus; and their brother Lazarus, who had fallen ill (v. 1).

Chapter 11 and the story of Lazarus reminds me of stories I've heard of medical mistaken identity. While the story of Lazarus's family isn't about misidentification, it can help us better understand the deep grief of losing a loved one and the overwhelming joy of finding out that loved one is actually alive.

Let me explain what I mean. Occurrences of mistaken identity in the health care world are not unique; they have been the story of too many people, unfortunately, too many times. Mistaken identity occurs when one person's identity is swapped with another's, sometimes during an accident. The trauma of misidentification, while intriguing, is also tragic, and has been re-created in a number of movies and books. Heart-wrenching details unfold as people are incorrectly identified after accidents. Victims' identities are swapped, and one person is taken unconscious to the hospital while the other is pronounced dead. These types of grave mistakes wreak havoc among family members on both sides. Consider a family who is told by the authorities that their loved one didn't survive. Intense grief sets in as they begin to process their loss and go through the motions of laying their dear one to rest. But then, they find out hours, days, or in some cases, even weeks later that the one they love is actually alive. Can you imagine how jolting the swing of emotions must feel?

As Lazarus's condition grew worse, Mary and Martha sent word to Jesus. They believed that if He would come, He could heal their cherished brother. But when Jesus received word, He showed no urgency in going to Lazarus. He simply said, "This illness does not lead to death. It is for the glory of God, so that the Son of God may be glorified through it" (v. 4). Jesus then said to the disciples, "Our friend Lazarus has fallen asleep, but I go to awaken him" (v. 11). Jesus was speaking of Lazarus's death, but the disciples misunderstood His meaning and thought He was referring to literal sleep. Jesus responded—and I wonder if He wanted to roll His eyes at their inability to comprehend—"Lazarus has died" (v. 14).

When He was ready to go to Lazarus, Jesus set out for Bethany, back in Judea, where there were threats against Him. Before His arrival, He was met by Martha and learned that Lazarus had been buried four days earlier. We're told that the disciples, along with Mary and Martha, believed that if Jesus had arrived sooner, Lazarus would have still been alive (vv. 21, 32, 37). Martha poured out her heart to Him, and although she did not understand, He responded, "Your brother will rise again" (v. 23). In the midst of her deep sadness, Martha continued to profess her faith in Jesus as God's Son, all while struggling to make sense of her grief in light of her faith. We know she was crushed, and maybe she even felt betrayed that Jesus had not arrived in time to help. But as we have seen so many times during Jesus's life, as well as today, He had different timing and a different plan, one that made sense only to Him.

Even though Jesus knew what He was preparing to do, He was overcome with emotion when He saw His friends weeping. "He was deeply moved in his spirit and greatly troubled" (v. 33). We're told He actually wept with them (v. 35). Surely this must have been curious to the people. Why hadn't He chosen to arrive in time to save His friend? Only Jesus and His Father knew the stunning miracle that was about to take place.

Approaching the tomb where Lazarus had been laid to rest, Jesus directed those with Him to remove the stone from the cave's entrance. Jesus cried out loudly, "Lazarus, come out" (v. 43). And then we see something truly unbelievable. "The man who had died came out, his hands and feet bound with linen strips, and his face wrapped with a cloth. Jesus said to them, 'Unbind him, and let him go'" (v. 44). Because of Jesus, Lazarus was alive! Death was defeated as He commanded Lazarus to come forth from the dark tomb. Surely Mary's and Martha's tears continued to flow, turning from tears of sadness to tears of joy. Much like the families in the stories of mistaken identity, Lazarus's loved ones must have felt an indescribable and unbelievable swing of emotion.

The story of Lazarus's resurrection precedes yet another humanly impossible event, which we celebrate on Easter morning. Of course, we're talking about the resurrection of Jesus! Like Lazarus's death, Jesus's death was met by tears of grief from those who loved Him, and like Lazarus's resurrection, Jesus's resurrection was met by tears of joy, awe, and jubilant celebration. When life conquers death, emotions flow and words simply cannot describe the triumph.

As humans we are prone to doubt. In the story of Lazarus, we see that God's timing doesn't always make sense. But He always comes through, for His glory. Trusting in His timing and His love for us changes who we are. It changes our entire mindset. We no longer have to doubt when life doesn't make sense. We can have the confidence that a loving God, whose plan for us is perfect, will provide for and protect us. As a result of Jesus's death and resurrection, in Him, we are fully *alive*. The day we place our faith in Him, our souls are released from sin and shame. No longer bound by darkness, we take off our grave clothes and rejoice. Our Savior has conquered death on our behalf, and with Him, we are saved.

Promise

Blessed be the God and Father of our Lord Jesus Christ! According to his great mercy, he has caused us to be born again to a living hope through the resurrection of Jesus Christ from the dead. (1 Peter 1:3)

John 11
Alive, Part 2

What a powerful story of foreshadowing we find in John chapter 11. As we see Jesus bring life back into Lazarus's body, we are invited to also see God resurrecting the dead places in our own lives. But He doesn't just resurrect us; He sits with us in grief and sadness. He understands us more than anyone on earth possibly can. He took on loneliness and death when He was separated from His Father, when He breathed His last breath on the cross saying, "It is finished" (John 19:30). Because of this, we know that He can sympathize with us in our sad and lonely places. As we read the story of Lazarus, we have hope, believing that God can do anything, even bring the dead back to life.

Process

1. When certain circumstances worry and overwhelm you and your prayers seem to go unheard, how does that make you feel about God?
2. What is one thing in your life today that you can't understand?
3. Do you remember a time in your past when you had trouble trusting God's timing, but He eventually showed Himself faithful?
4. Why is it so difficult to surrender to God when things aren't going in the direction you had hoped?

5. What emotions are stirred within when you realize that Jesus is weeping with you in the darkest and most painful places of your life?

Prayer

Dear heavenly Father, this resurrection story is quite unbelievable to me. When I grasp the implications of what Jesus can do in the life of an individual, it is both overwhelming and inviting. Thank You that when I cry, You cry with me. Thank You that when I feel deep grief, You grieve with me. Sometimes I find it so difficult to trust Your timing. Give me the strength to have confidence in Your plan for me. Thank You that the things in life that feel hopeless and dead can be brought back to life because of what Your Son, Jesus, did on the cross. Today, I jubilantly celebrate Your loving concern for me.

Promises

I will recount the steadfast love of the LORD,
   the praises of the LORD,
according to all that the LORD has granted us,
   and the great goodness to the house of Israel
that he has granted them according to his compassion,
   according to the abundance of his steadfast love. (Isaiah 63:7)

And you were dead in the trespasses and sins in which you once walked, following the course of this world, following the prince of the power of the air, the spirit that is now at work in the sons of disobedience—among whom we all once lived in the passions of our flesh, carrying out the desires of the body and the mind, and were by nature children of wrath, like the rest of mankind. But God, being rich in mercy, because of the great love with which he loved us, even when we were dead in our trespasses, made us alive together with Christ—by grace you have been saved. (Ephesians 2:1–5)

For if while we were enemies we were reconciled to God by the death of his Son, much more, now that we are reconciled, shall we be saved by his life. (Romans 5:10)

John 12
Honored, Part 1

So they took branches of palm trees and went out to meet him, crying out, "Hosanna! Blessed is he who comes in the name of the Lord, even the King of Israel!"
—John 12:13

I remember my only daughter's wedding as if it were yesterday. At the end of the traditional first dance between bride and groom, my husband took our beautiful, newly married daughter into his arms for the father-bride dance. He couldn't take his eyes off her. With love and emotion covering his face, he guided his beloved daughter across the dance floor with grace and charm. This dance represented the transition from the relationship they had always known. As they reflected on wonderful memories, they were filled with affection for each other. He held her in high esteem before our family and friends. But it was not only my husband's eyes that were glowing that day; my daughter's were alight as well. She adored her dad. During those few moments together on the dance floor, she silently expressed gratitude for the man that had given her so much. We were moved to tears as we watched father and daughter regard one another. It was impossible to tell at that moment who was more honored, the father or the bride.

Honored means regarded with great respect or esteem. In John 12, we step into two scenes of people honoring Jesus, the King of all kings. In the first narrative, we find Jesus in the home of siblings Mary, Martha, and the newly risen Lazarus. He had come to their home in Bethany where they were preparing dinner for Him. The joy of having Lazarus back from the dead and reclining at the table with his Savior must have been overwhelming! We're told that Martha served the meal while Mary took an expensive ointment, anointed Jesus's feet, and then wiped them with her hair (v. 3). The perfume's fragrance and the spirit of celebration filled the air. One of Jesus's disciples—Judas Iscariot, who was soon to betray Him—took issue with Mary's actions, saying the ointment should have been sold to benefit the poor. After Judas devalued Mary's act of worship, Jesus rebuked him. "Leave her alone, so that she may keep it for the day of my burial" (v. 7). In that moment, Mary only wanted to honor Him as her Lord, and Jesus received the gesture with grace.

In the second narrative, we find an inspirational illustration of honor as Jesus returned to Jerusalem on a donkey's back. The onlookers waved palm branches and shouted with joy because finally, Jesus, their long-awaited King, had arrived. This return, or triumphal entry, has become a part of the Easter celebration, the day we call Palm Sunday, and marks the beginning of Holy Week. The events that unfold during the week preceding Easter carry deep meaning and significance to believers. And while most know about the darkness of the crucifixion, Palm Sunday is a day of hope and rejoicing.

By this time in Jesus's ministry, people had likely heard the stories of His miracles and His parables or witnessed them firsthand. Proof had been provided for those who'd been longing to believe He was the Savior. When they saw Him ride in on a donkey, they shouted, "Hosanna! Blessed is he who comes in the name of the Lord, even the King of Israel!" (vv. 13–14). The Greek and Hebrew origins of the word *hosanna* literally mean "please come and save us." Some remembered the prophesied words, "Fear not, daughter of Zion; behold, your king is coming, sitting on a donkey's colt!" (v. 15). To many, seeing Jesus riding in on a colt eased their fear that the Savior might never come. The time was near, and soon He would be revealed as their long-awaited King.

But while Jesus knew what lay ahead, the people did not. As He watched them celebrate His arrival, He must have been filled with sadness—sadness for the difficult days to come and sadness for what the unknowing people were about to witness. But He also knew that ultimately, this would not be the end of the story. "And Jesus answered them, 'The hour has come for the Son of Man to be glorified. Truly, truly, I say to you, unless a grain of wheat falls into the earth and dies, it remains alone; but if it dies, it bears much fruit. Whoever loves his life loses it, and whoever hates his life in this world will keep it for eternal life'" (vv. 23–25). He knew an explanation of the upcoming events wouldn't make sense at that time, but He was trying to prepare them for the fact that His death would not mean all was lost. His death would actually lead to new life. But these brothers and sisters would not fully understand what was happening until after His death—the third day after, to be exact.

In this emotionally confusing moment, we can believe that Jesus is speaking to us as well. He is telling us that we, too, hold a place of honor in His sight. "If anyone serves me, he must follow me; and where I am, there will my servant be also. If anyone serves me, the Father will honor him" (v. 26). When we celebrate the victory won on the cross, how can we not feel highly regarded? God looks at us and sees His Son. Jesus made the ultimate sacrifice on our behalf. He has truly honored us by granting us a righteous record that we did not earn and do not deserve. In order to understand God's grace, it's important that we also understand His honor for us. Why would He forgive us time and again and offer us unconditional love? Because we belong to Him. We are His children. And just as a parent continues to love their child in good times as well as bad, God will always continue to love us, respect us, and yes, even hold us in high esteem.

In John 12, it's difficult to say who is more honored. The people honored Jesus when He rode into Jerusalem on a donkey. But He was about to honor them in a way they couldn't imagine. He was about to suffer and die on a cross for them, for us. He *honored* us, and in turn, we can honor Him by living a life which pleases Him. Let us express gratitude to Him, our father who has given us so much. May our eyes alight as we move through life one day at a time, regarding our heavenly Father and bringing glory to Him.

Promise

For those who honor me I will honor. (1 Samuel 2:30)

John 12
Honored, Part 2

As we read the stories of Jesus from the book of John, time and again we see people honor and respect Him in all sorts of ways. When like them, we truly embrace that Jesus is the Son of God, we too have the opportunity to honor Him as Savior and Lord. We also understand that Jesus honored us by going to the cross on our behalf. Acknowledging the sacrifice He made for us will bring a genuine desire to live our lives for Him. He honors us, and in turn, we can honor Him by living for and growing closer to Him every day. When we remember the people from the book of John and the many ways they honored Christ, may it be a reminder that we have this exact same opportunity to honor Him with our own lives.

Process

1. What emotions arise when you think of Mary washing Jesus's feet?
2. What emotions do you think filled the people along the streets as they waved palm branches?
3. Can you remember a time when you felt honored by someone?
4. Who is someone that you care about and can imagine honoring?
5. In response to all that God has done for you, what are some ways you can honor Him with your life?

Prayer

God, as I seek to honor and esteem You, I realize that You are calling me to surrender every part of my life to You. At times, my desire to be close to You is interrupted by my own earthly distractions. Help me to remember how You honored and esteemed me by not only adopting me as Your child but also sending Your son to die for me. I celebrate His victory on the cross. When I consider all the amazing things about You as my Father, I can't help but feel awe. Remind me once again today about Your spotless character and Your unconditional and unfailing love for me.

Promises

If anyone serves me, he must follow me; and where I am, there will my servant be also. If anyone serves me, the Father will honor him. (John 12:26)

So that the tested genuineness of your faith—more precious than gold that perishes though it is tested by fire—may be found to result in praise and glory and honor at the revelation of Jesus Christ. (1 Peter 1:7)

John 13
Served, Part 1

A new commandment I give to you, that you love one another: just as I have loved you, you also are to love one another.

—John 13:34

I work in health care. The health-care sector, from the inside, is a beautiful thing. We have some of the brightest and most caring people you will ever meet. These workers do not simply show up for their jobs; they show up to make a difference in people's lives. In 2020, when a pandemic hit, our health-care system was challenged. The frightening time of uncertainty brought with it conflicting medical information, and the new virus brought challenges and confusion regarding its prevention and treatment. Tension and dissent across the country and around the world ran high. As health-care workers, we, like most people, felt uncomfortable with the unknown, but even in the face of fear, we moved forward every day with the same purpose: to care for our patients.

Time has since passed, but there is one phenomenon, one particular feeling from those early days of the pandemic, that I will never forget. I'll always remember the way in which the people of our community, our administrators, and our physicians—all leaders in one way or another—came alongside the staff. Countless trinkets, signs, ribbons, and prayer vigils were offered in support of and appreciation for the health-care community. People made masks, brought special treats, and lauded health-care workers as heroes. One of our physicians personally provided catered lunches for the entire staff numerous times. In a heartfelt email—which I will never delete—another physician personally offered to provide medical care to any one of us who might contract the virus. During the pandemic, kindhearted people showed up again and again and again, each in their own way, to serve.

As is often the case, Jesus's actions in John 13 speak louder than His words. Here we see Jesus in a new light, one that illuminates His heart. He came to earth as Messiah, yet He fulfilled His mission by humbly serving others. Let's take a look at one specific way this Savior, this Son of God, demonstrated a humble willingness to serve.

The primary mode of transportation in Jesus's day was walking, and the shoes worn were sandals. The streets were dusty and sometimes lined with garbage and animal waste. Because of this, obviously, feet needed to be washed upon entering a home. Tables sat low to the floor, and guests reclined around them while eating. Clean feet would clearly have been preferable in this setting. In those times, the lowest-ranked servant in the home was tasked with washing visitors' feet upon arrival. This was a way for hosts to honor and serve their guests.

In the previous chapter, we saw Mary washing Jesus's feet with perfume. "Mary therefore took a pound of expensive ointment made from pure nard, and anointed the feet of Jesus and wiped his feet with her hair. The house was filled with the fragrance of the perfume" (John 12:3). But in this chapter, we see a role reversal. The disciples had gathered for a meal with Jesus, and although they did not know it, this was their last supper with Him. While they were eating, we're told Jesus rose from the table and did something unexpected. He took a towel, poured water into a basin, and began to wash each of His disciples' feet (vv. 4–5). Taking the role of the lowliest of servants, He thoughtfully and carefully performed this act, honoring each one around the table. By washing their feet, Jesus demonstrated how He valued them. Jesus said, "The Son of Man came not to be served but to serve" (Matthew 20:28; Mark 10:45). Although He was the Son of God, He didn't rule over His people with an iron fist. Instead, He served them. He became one of them, walked with them, shared meals with them, cried with them, and most of all, He loved them. He wanted them to understand that believing in Him was not a religious practice but a warm invitation into a meaningful relationship with Him. His love for them was beautifully expressed through this humble act. One day Jesus was having His feet washed by Mary, and the next, He was washing the feet of His disciples. One day He was being served and worshipped; the next day He was serving others.

When Jesus came to wash the feet of Peter, he refused Him saying, "You shall never wash my feet." But Jesus answered, "If I do not wash you, you have no share with me" (v. 8). Jesus was preparing the disciples for the coming days, the days of His death, and although they could not yet understand, He was showing them that a much more significant type of washing lay ahead. By dying, He was going to wash away their sin. You may have heard the phrase "washed in the blood of the Lamb." Because of the sacrifice Jesus made on the cross, our imperfect record has been replaced with His perfect one. He drapes His robe of righteousness over our shoulders, covering our sin. The moment we accept Him, we are forgiven. His blood washes away our sin—past, present, and future—and because of Him, we are clean.

Have you accepted what Jesus offers? Have you allowed Him to metaphorically wash your feet? Much like our community came together to serve the health-care workers during the recent pandemic, Jesus came to *serve* His people. By humbly and symbolically washing their feet, He honored them. If you accept Him, you will be received into His family, forgiven and honored, and you'll experience the privilege of living a fulfilling life in service and honor to Him.

Promise
For our sake he made him to be sin who knew no sin, so that in him we might become the righteousness of God. (2 Corinthians 5:21)

John 13
Served, Part 2

It seems as if Jesus's words are usually accompanied by a personal illustration from His own life. In this chapter, Jesus's humility shines bright and clear and allows us to see some of the softest places in His heart. The picture of Jesus washing His disciples' feet illustrates how much He cared for and valued them. How kind of God to send His Son to earth with compassion rather than a heavy iron fist. Jesus presented Himself to the people with a humble, gentle spirit as He walked with them, shared meals with them, served them, and cried with them. The people must have felt more important to Him than we can imagine.

Process
1. How does the thought of Jesus washing your feet like He washed the disciples' make you feel?
2. Do you see Jesus as a distant friend or one with whom you are emotionally connected?
3. What do you think might inhibit a close connection with God?
4. What does it mean to you that Jesus not only paid the penalty for your sin, but He also gives you daily and eternal grace?
5. Consider writing a prayer of gratitude for the way Jesus has and will always serve you.

Prayer

Father God, as You drape Your robe of righteousness over my shoulders I realize that You are covering my sin. Help me to daily accept You and remember that You have forgiven me. Jesus's blood washes away all of my sins—past, present, and future—and because of Him, I am clean. I want to receive the spiritual gifts that You offer me. Allow me to accept the thought of Jesus humbly washing my feet, cleansing me. I'm so thankful to be a part of Your family, to have the opportunity to live a fulfilling life because of what You have done for me.

Promises

And walk in love, as Christ loved us and gave himself up for us, a fragrant offering and sacrifice to God. (Ephesians 5:2)

And this is his commandment, that we believe in the name of his Son Jesus Christ and love one another, just as he has commanded us. (1 John 3:23)

Beloved, let us love one another, for love is from God, and whoever loves has been born of God and knows God. (1 John 4:7)

John 14
Nurtured, Part 1

Peace I leave with you; my peace I give to you. Not as the world gives do I give to you. Let not your hearts be troubled, neither let them be afraid.

—John 14:27

Sunlight pierces the room, awakening you. You slowly open your eyes and see unfamiliar surroundings taking shape. Details of a new place come to light. Something feels warm and welcoming. It's the heavenly smell coming from the kitchen. The rich aromas of coffee brewing and bacon sizzling bring a smile to your face. Someone is thinking about you, preparing breakfast for you, providing care and hospitality for you. Being a welcomed guest, whether as a friend in someone's home or a customer at a lovely inn in the mountains, can bring such a restful feeling. It's wonderful having someone receive and nurture you.

In John 14, Jesus's horrendous suffering and crucifixion were drawing near. He would hang on a cross, rise from the dead, and later depart from earth and ascend to heaven. We see His kindness as He longed to prepare the disciples for all the difficulties ahead. He knew the intense days would be deeply troubling. "And now I have told you before it takes place, so that when it does take place you may believe. I will no longer talk much with you" (vv. 29–30). The chapter opens with Jesus's warm and welcoming words to His disciples. Surely He felt their discomfort with all of the unrest swirling around them. We can only imagine how intriguing and unpredictable life with Jesus had been. The disciples must have eagerly anticipated each day with Him. They surely looked forward to finding out what the next day serving Jesus would bring. Even with all the controversy surrounding Him, Jesus's presence made them feel safe. But the disciples couldn't fathom why He would leave them or where He was planning to go. Jesus foretold His departure, but at the same time, He assured them that there was a specific reason for it.

We read a lot of dialogue in this chapter as Jesus prepared His disciples for a life without Him. He gave the reason for leaving in verses 2 and 3. "In my Father's house are many rooms. If it were not so, would I have told you that I go to prepare a place for you? And if I go and prepare a place for you, I will come again and will take you to myself, that where I am you may be also." He also provided clear instruction about how they were to live after He was gone. "If you love me, you will keep my commandments" (v. 15). At the same time, He reassured them that He would not be leaving them alone but would give them a Helper. This had to be difficult, if not impossible, to understand. "And I will ask the Father, and he will give you another Helper, to be with you forever" (v. 16). But consider the most important words He spoke to them. Addressing Thomas, "Jesus said to him, 'I am the way, and the truth, and the life. No one comes to the Father except through me'" (v. 6). He continued explaining, in a number of different ways, that the path to God was through Himself. His followers must have been wondering what this meant. They did not yet understand that this was an invitation. He invited the people time and again to believe in the One who had sent Him. Each of them was welcomed into His family as an adopted son or daughter to be forgiven, nurtured, and loved. "I will not leave you as orphans; I will come to you" (v. 18).

When my grandson was a toddler, he would often get afraid at night or when his parents took him to childcare. My son and his wife would ease his fears with the following statement: "Mama and Daddy always come back." They would repeat it over and over and over again. They taught him to repeat it to himself whenever he felt alone or was afraid. And of course, they always kept that promise. They always came back. Believing this, he could remain calm and brave.

In a simple way, this picture reminds us of how God cares tenderly for us. He knows that at times we find it hard to believe that He is near. Our minds often wonder about the future, and doubts arise. God understands our fears. He loves to reassure us. And although we still sometimes feel alone or afraid, He is always there for us. Jesus continued explaining about the Helper that God would send. "Even the Spirit of truth, whom the world cannot receive, because it neither sees him nor knows him. You know him, for he dwells with you and will be in you" (v. 17). It gives God great pleasure to provide His presence at all times for His children through the Holy Spirit.

Remember the sheep that followed their shepherd because they recognized his voice? Jesus's message of love and care for His people is a focus in both chapter 10 and here again in chapter 14. Did you know that sheep cannot lie down and rest until they are well fed and feel protected by their shepherd? Jesus said in verse 27, "Peace I leave with you; my peace I give to you. Not as the world gives do I give to you. Let not your hearts be troubled, neither let them be afraid." This message was not only for the disciples but also for us today. He wants us to feel His care and protection. He wants us to feel His presence through the Holy Spirit, the Helper. The next time we feel anxious, afraid, or forsaken, let's remember some of Jesus's last words on the cross: "My God, my God, why have you forsaken me?" (Matthew 27:46). He understands what it feels like to be alone. But God's Word expresses countless times how deeply the Father cares for us by never leaving us. His constant love and continual presence remind us that we are *nurtured*, cherished children of God, and He is preparing a place for us in heaven where we will be together forever.

Promise
And behold, I am with you always, to the end of the age. (Matthew 28:20)

John 14
Nurtured, Part 2

Over time, we have seen Jesus grow closer and closer to His disciples. Jesus had many touching conversations with His friends, guiding them gently into conversation, which included kind instruction and encouragement. Deeply connected to His brothers, surely Jesus was beginning to feel a great sadness at the thought of leaving them. He may have known they would feel abandoned. These emotions are expressed in the fourteenth chapter of John when He begins to tell them that although He might not always be with them, He would always take care of them. Like the disciples, we too can be assured that He will never leave us alone, but He will take care of us by providing a Helper to be with us forever. This constant presence, this Holy Spirit of God, will stay with us, bringing power and peace throughout our lives.

Process
1. Does God feel near to you as He promises, or does He feel distant?
2. What is one practical way that you can be reminded of God's presence?
3. Do you remember a time when you felt welcomed by God?
4. Explain how your acknowledgment of God's presence gives you peace.
5. Find and write out a verse in the Bible that reminds you of the promise of His presence.

Prayer

God, whenever I acknowledge You in my life, I receive an overwhelming sense of peace. Thank You that I'm not, nor will I ever be alone. Thank You for always being with me. Please remind me of how perfectly You take care of me. Sometimes my mind fills with doubt and fear, and I find it hard to believe that You are nearby. Thank You for continually reassuring me through the presence of Your Holy Spirit.

Promises

No man will be able to stand before you all the days of your life. Just as I was with Moses, so I will be with you. I will not leave you or forsake you. (Joshua 1:5)

The LORD of hosts is with us;
   the God of Jacob is our fortress. (Psalm 46:7)

For where two or three are gathered in my name, there am I among them. (Matthew 18:20)

John 15
Connected, Part 1

I am the vine; you are the branches. Whoever abides in me and I in him, he it is that bears much fruit, for apart from me you can do nothing.

—John 15:5

Discovering one's heritage can be fascinating. There's something intriguing about ancestry. Uncovering new revelations from past generations is often eye-opening and revealing. I remember my grandmother drawing our family tree on enormous pieces of thick, white paper that she spread over her dining room table. She spent countless hours researching countless documents in order to find her connections to the past. She was proud of the fact that we might have British royalty in our blood, and although she was never able to finalize the royal connection, she was convinced this was true. I believe it made her feel validated to know she was a part of a regal bloodline.

While having ancestry information readily available can be wonderful, it can also cause problems. People sometimes find delightful connections in their family trees or even discover unexpected financial inheritances. But others might find information that leads to disappointment or even shame. Our identity can be positively or negatively affected, and even altered forever, when we uncover our roots.

In chapter 15 of John, Jesus's time on earth was coming to an end. He was well aware that His crucifixion was drawing near. It couldn't have been easy, but with confidence in His Father's plan, He continued teaching the disciples, trying to help them understand what was happening and why. The disciples had become a sort of band of brothers, strong and unified. They had formed bonds that likely made them feel like family, with Jesus at the helm.

Jesus knew that His disciples, like many of us, struggled with their identities. He longed for them to understand His family tree. God was His Father and *He* was God's Son, and if they chose to connect with Him, they too would be part of God's family. They would be His children. So Jesus explained the concept of identity by talking about a literal vine and its branches. He told the disicples that branches only bear fruit when connected to a vine, and He went on to say that He was the vine that offered life to the branches. "I am the true vine, and my Father is the vinedresser" (v. 1). This illustration demonstrated how the branch was a part of the whole, and apart from the vine, the branches wouldn't be able to bear fruit (v. 4). In Jesus's own words, "Apart from me you can do nothing" (v. 5). This was a warm invitation to His disciples, and to us, to discover a place on His family tree, one that provides a life of fruitfulness and joy.

Jesus beautifully weaves the conversation with themes of love. "As the Father has loved me, so have I loved you. Abide in my love" (v. 9). This was the key to a relationship with Him. Staying connected to the vine would create an identity in Him and result in being accepted and cherished as a member of His family. Full of His love and grace, the disciples then would be able to pour out the same love and grace to a world in need. "This is my commandment, that you love one another as I have loved you. Greater love has no one than this, that someone lay down his life for his friends" (vv. 12–13).

The phrase "identity in Christ" might sound like a Christian cliché. For many, it's challenging to clearly understand and put this concept into words. Identity is about more than an association with a family; it's about becoming a member of a family. Once a person becomes a member of a family, the connection is permanent. Additionally, our families define us and play key roles in who we become. Staying connected to family provides security and comfort. Staying connected to Jesus provides permanent and deep-rooted security. If we are children of God, He defines who we are and who we will become, and we will forever be related to Him.

As believers, or children of God, what is our heritage? When we trust Jesus as Savior, we are given the opportunity to become a member of God's family. Being a part of His family is rich with reward. He offers forgiveness, hope, and perfect love. He has defined us once and for all. But staying closely *connected* in relationship to Him is key, because apart from Him we are inadequate and incomplete (v. 5). Talk to Him, listen to Him, grow closer to Him. If you have not already, would you consider joining His family today? He has extended an invitation for you to find delightful connections in His family tree and discover unexpected and eternal spiritual inheritances. He loves you. He wants to be here for you, to have a meaningful and continuous connection with you. May we begin now and always find our identity in Him, our Father, the one who loves us like no other.

Promise

It is the LORD who goes before you. He will be with you; he will not leave you or forsake you. (Deuteronomy 31:8)

John 15
Connected, Part 2

It's difficult to imagine the emotions that Jesus must have felt as His crucifixion drew near, but trusting God's plan for Him gave Him the strength He needed to press forward. His disciples witnessed Him set the perfect example of faith and obedience. His uninterrupted connection with His Father gave Him the confidence and strength to step into this daunting story. When we, like Jesus, believe in God as our loving Father and trust that His plans are best, we will also receive the strength we need to live with bravery and confidence that God has written a beautiful ending to our story.

Process
1. What is the most difficult area of your life to place in God's hands?
2. Can you remember a time when your life didn't make sense but later God revealed His good plan?
3. What distracts you from focusing on God?
4. How can you stay connected to God?
5. Do you know someone who may be having trouble trusting God? How could you encourage that person today?

Prayer
My dear Father, thank You so much that the heritage You have given me cannot be taken away. It is an honor and blessing to be a part of Your family. Thank You for offering me forgiveness, hope,

and most of all, Your perfect unending love. You have defined me once and for all. May I stay closely connected to You, always talking and listening to You, because apart from You I can do nothing. I long to continue to grow closer to You. Wrap my identity and security in what Your Word says about me. No matter what challenges come my way, help me always remember I'm chosen and cherished by You.

Promises

But now that you have been set free from sin and have become slaves of God, the fruit you get leads to sanctification and its end, eternal life. (Romans 6:22)

I can do all things through him who strengthens me.
(Philippians 4:13)

But grow in the grace and knowledge of our Lord and Savior Jesus Christ. To him be the glory both now and to the day of eternity. Amen. (2 Peter 3:18)

John 16
Prepared, Part 1

When the Spirit of truth comes, he will guide you into all the truth, for he will not speak on his own authority, but whatever he hears he will speak, and he will declare to you the things that are to come.

—John 16:13

The journey to the cross continued as conversations between Jesus and His friends grew somber, but never without a word of hope from the Savior. His call for them to believe in Him as Messiah was coupled with the explanation that this very belief would involve risk. "I have said all these things to you to keep you from falling away. They will put you out of the synagogues. Indeed, the hour is coming when whoever kills you will think he is offering service to God. And they will do these things because they have not known the Father, nor me" (vv. 1–3).

With the short time remaining, Jesus spoke with heartfelt passion. "But I have said these things to you, that when their hour comes you may remember that I told them to you" (v. 4). With His words, He prepared the disciples for the feelings of confusion, loneliness, and helplessness that were just around the corner. "But because I have said these things to you, sorrow has filled your heart" (v. 6). He had been there to help them, and while He had experienced the presence of the Spirit, they had not. Little did they know, they were about to receive this powerful and

Holy Spirit of God. They were about to be accompanied by an ever-present aid and companion. But for a moment, they would be left alone. "I came from the Father and have come into the world, and now I am leaving the world and going to the Father" (v. 28).

I once heard someone say, "The older I get, the more my parents make sense." Now that my sons are adults, I can say this with conviction. Raising children, while completely wonderful, can also be mentally trying and physically exhausting. As a parent, the responsibility is enormous. There are so many life lessons to teach our kids and so many dangers about which to warn them. I remember one particular time when my boys were very small, two were preschoolers and one a baby, and I needed to pick up a couple of things at a department store. We walked in the store and my little boys took off running in different directions, hiding under the endless racks of clothing, scaring me to death. It was time to teach them about staying close beside me in public places, and although they didn't fully understand why, they had to trust me.

Several years later, they were in middle school, and they understood about the dangers of small children getting separated from their parents, but there were new things they needed to learn. Around this time, energy drinks loaded with caffeine hit the market. We had to have a conversation about caffeine and its effects on young hearts and bodies. They had to trust me about the danger, even though they really wanted to drink energy drinks nonstop with their friends late into the night.

Not too much time passed, and my boys understood and had seen the negative effects of energy drinks. They were now in high school, and it was time they learned to drive. We had to explain to them that even if there were no other cars around, they couldn't drift into the other person's lane. Here, again, they had to trust me with something they couldn't fully understand. But soon, after a short time on the road, they got it. Teaching our boys practical life lessons was vital to their safety and well-being, but they couldn't learn these important lessons until they were ready.

Jesus taught His disciples many truths that were extremely difficult, even impossible for them to understand. Many times, they simply had to trust Him. They couldn't fully comprehend all the things about which He spoke, but they listened and processed and trusted His words. As His followers leaned in to learn, Jesus equipped them mentally and emotionally for the days ahead.

There was no need for Jesus to prepare the disciples for His final hours too far in advance. He gave them the information they needed only when the time was right. "I did not say these things to you from the beginning, because I was with you" (v. 4). But He knew that He was about to leave. "Nevertheless, I tell you the truth: it is to your advantage that I go away, for if I do not go away, the Helper will not come to you. But if I go, I will send him to you" (v. 7). How His heart must have gone out to them, His friends for whom He cared so deeply. He perceived their needs in a supernatural way. While on earth, His own assurance came from experiencing the presence of His Father's Spirit. "Yet I am not alone, for the Father is with me" (v. 32). The Holy Spirit's presence gave Him peace and assurance, and He knew the Spirit would do the same for them. "He will glorify me, for he will take what is mine and declare it to you" (v. 14).

Jesus stated very clearly that His time on earth was nearing its end. "A little while, and you will see me no longer" (v. 16). Confusion coupled with anxiety filled the disciples, and they began questioning one another. "We do not know what he is talking about" (v. 18). We can only imagine how helpless they felt. But as always, He assured them that after He was gone, His Holy Spirit would continue to care for them. This new Spirit would offer help, provide comfort, and enable them to have an ongoing relationship with God through His constant presence. With the promise of His Spirit, Jesus *prepared* them for a new kind of life filled with unimaginable peace. "You will be sorrowful, but your sorrow will turn into joy" (v. 20). His Spirit would always remain alongside them, providing contentment despite their circumstances.

The disciples couldn't always understand Jesus's reasoning, just like my young sons couldn't always understand mine. But this is life. This is learning truth over time. Having faith means opening our mind to things we don't yet understand. Sometimes life doesn't make sense, but we can move ahead with God's Spirit by our side, believing He knows what's best for us. In time, God will reveal all things and we will understand His ways. Let's believe in what we cannot yet comprehend and trust in His perfect plan, His perfect timing, and most of all, His perfect love.

Promise

I have said these things to you, that in me you may have peace. In the world you will have tribulation. But take heart; I have overcome the world. (John 16:33)

John 16
Prepared, Part 2

John 16 echoes a similar theme from the previous chapter—Jesus preparing the disciples for His departure. It seems as if He was slowly revealing information to His followers over time, only when they were ready. Can you imagine their confusion coupled with their anxiety as they began to understand that He was preparing to leave them? They must have felt helpless, but as always, Jesus reassured them that His Holy Spirit would continue to empower them when He was gone. His Spirit would remain with them, providing help and comfort and enabling them to have a meaningful relationship with God their Father. This promise must have offered them hope. We, like the disciples, sometimes experience feelings of confusion, loneliness, and helplessness when we don't feel that God is near. But His Spirit is always near and always available to us whenever we call out to Him.

Process
1. What negative emotions are you struggling with today?
2. Do you feel as if you are having to work through things on your own?
3. Remind yourself about and thank God for His Spirit that Jesus offered the disciples and you.
4. How would you define the word *companion*?
5. Do you see God as a distant being who is an acquaintance, or can you believe that He dwells with you at all times?

Prayer

Jesus, I understand the power and presence of Your Holy Spirit who is always with me. Much like the disciples, I sometimes feel overwhelmed by life's ups and downs. I want to trust You more. Will You help me? My faith seems so weak at times. How I long to comprehend all of the security that comes with a greater awareness of who You truly are. Thank You for never leaving me. Thank You for equipping me to mentally and emotionally face the unknown future. Would You grow my faith stronger, especially when life doesn't make sense? I know that I can trust You. Help me live accordingly, believing this is true today.

Promises

For everyone who has been born of God overcomes the world. And this is the victory that has overcome the world—our faith. (1 John 5:4)

Now may the Lord of peace himself give you peace at all times in every way. The Lord be with you all. (2 Thessalonians 3:16)

And the peace of God, which surpasses all understanding, will guard your hearts and your minds in Christ Jesus. (Philippians 4:7)

John 17
Protected, Part 1

I in them and you in me, that they may become per-
fectly one, so that the world may know that you sent
me and loved them even as you loved me.

—John 17:23

My husband and I own a coffee shop. We regularly offer pop-up opportunities for local artists to display and sell their work. From books and canvas to jewelry and sculpture, we love displaying the handmade and heartfelt work of creative people from around our city. One morning I noticed a young woman walking into the shop escorting an older lady, maybe in her 70s. Curious looks covered their faces. I could tell by their expressions that this was their first time in our shop. They glanced from the menu to the customers, taking in the "lay of the land." But these women were not interested in ordering coffee. They headed to the bar, taking their seats on two barstools, clearly eager to chat. I quickly discovered that the older lady was an artist—a potter—and she and her friend had heard about our pop-up shop opportunities. The younger woman began to explain that because of family challenges, her friend had not had the opportunity to display this pottery. She had been spinning a potter's wheel for decades. Her collection had grown over time, and many handmade pieces now sat stacked on her garage shelves.

When I asked if they had brought any samples of her work along, they dashed out to the car and returned carrying a tattered cardboard box filled with old newspapers. I had no idea what lay inside. I knew the pottery pieces were treasures to these women, but would I, or others, feel the same? No words can express my pleasant surprise as they began to reveal the newspaper-wrapped treasures. They brought out beautifully glazed teacups, candlesticks made of clay, little lambs with hand-painted expressions, and more. With delight and a bit of remorse, I exclaimed, "You've never shown these to anyone?" She shook her head.

Then she began to tell me her story—one that had been filled with hardship. Over time, her art had been a form of therapy. Over the years, she had encountered tough times, and escaping to her garage, spinning the wheel, forming the clay, and baking her carefully formed pieces had helped her cope. It had provided a welcome diversion and distraction. She had created dozens of pieces over time, and she'd kept them on her garage shelves, in pristine condition. How precious it was to watch her face light up as she saw the joy her pieces could bring to others. She finally had the opportunity to share her art, and we were privileged to have been a small part of making that happen. We were so amazed and thankful she had kept the precious handmade pieces safe for so long.

Prized, cherished, cared for, and protected. These are the concepts we receive from the seventeenth chapter of John. This chapter contains a beautiful prayer that Jesus prayed at the conclusion of the Last Supper, just before His arrest. At first glance, it seems Jesus was praying for His followers, but upon closer examination, it's clear He is praying for all believers, including us (v. 9). Have you ever considered the fact that Jesus prays for you? The thought of this is both poignant and moving. With a spirit of humility and gratitude, let's dare to imagine ourselves as the subject of what has been so aptly titled "The High Priestly Prayer."

Chapters 16 and 17 of John intersect when Jesus's conversation concerning the hardships of this world converges with His powerful prayer. This was His tender farewell. He was commending His beloved followers to God His Father, asking Him to keep them safe (17:15). Those for whom He was praying were not only partners in the faith, they were also His friends, and He cared deeply for them.

Jesus was only hours away from taking His daunting journey to the cross. He would soon be alone. His followers would not be able to rescue Him during His heinous persecution and death on the cross. Yes, they all needed prayer. He needed help from His Father to make it through the unthinkable torture ahead. His followers—who faced their own threats from His enemies—would need help as they prepared to witness their Messiah endure such torture. Jesus's High Priestly Prayer, also known as The Farewell Prayer, covered all of this.

Why, over the centuries, has this chapter been called "The High Priestly Prayer"? Up to this point in time, the only way for people to receive forgiveness for their sins was to engage with the high priest. They were required to go to the temple, verbally confess their sins to the priest, and make an animal sacrifice. Only after this process was complete were they allowed to connect with God. "For every high priest chosen from among men is appointed to act on behalf of men in relation to God, to offer gifts and sacrifices for sins" (Hebrews 5:1). This High Priestly Prayer that came from the mouth of Jesus Himself is filled with foreshadowing of the "great exchange," which would soon take place. He was about to become the ultimate sacrifice as He hung on the cross. It would no longer be necessary for us, as believers, to approach the high priest and individually offer sacrificial animals in order to connect with God. From that point forward, they were covered by Jesus's blood. Jesus's perfection would stand in the place of their sin, and they would be able to directly approach God and receive His grace.

The rituals once required to approach God are no longer necessary. Jesus has replaced the human high priest and become the mediator between God and man, interceding on our behalf. "But if anyone does sin, we have an advocate with the Father, Jesus Christ the righteous" (1 John 2:1). The prospect of death on a cross would have been unbearable aside from the knowledge that all God's children would forever be free to approach Him. Jesus prayed to His Father in verse 10, "All mine are yours, and yours are mine, and I am glorified in them." This is a clear statement, even a declaration of who we are in relation to Christ. What a beautiful prayer Jesus prayed for them and for us.

Much like my new potter friend had created and treasured her works of art, Jesus created and treasures us. We have been beautifully crafted, and we are deeply cared for by Him. He loves us and prizes us simply because we are His. We are cherished and *protected* by Him until the day we will be presented before God because of Jesus, spotless and clean.

Promise
Who is to condemn? Christ Jesus is the one who died—more than that, who was raised—who is at the right hand of God, who indeed is interceding for us. (Romans 8:34)

John 17
Protected, Part 2

Everyone wants to feel prized, cherished, and protected. John 17 portrays a beautiful picture of a secure identity. In The High Priestly Prayer, we hear Jesus's words of affirmation that He is praying over His followers. If we believe in Him, we can count on the fact that these words are prayed over us as well. Can you believe that Jesus prays especially for you? Imagine how tender His voice must have sounded as He prayed for those He loved. He cares just as deeply for you and me. We can unite with a very holy God, not because of anything we've done but because of what Jesus has done. His perfect record has replaced our imperfect one. One day we will be presented to God spotless and clean because of what Jesus did for us.

Process
1. In what areas of your life do you feel insecure or vulnerable?
2. Is there someone in your life who has affirmed you?
3. How does it feel when you hear that Jesus cherishes you?
4. What is your response to God as you feel His affirmations for you?
5. Whom do you know that needs to feel the love of God?

Prayer
Dear Jesus, thank You for creating me and treasuring me beyond what I can understand. You have beautifully, purposefully, and uniquely crafted me. Help me to see myself as You see me. Your

love for me deeply touches my heart. Your grace covers my imperfections every single time. When I don't believe I am cherished by You, I begin to feel worthless and insecure. Help me believe today that I am beloved and nothing can take that away.

Promises

But God shows his love for us in that while we were still sinners, Christ died for us. (Romans 5:8)

So that Christ may dwell in your hearts through faith—that you, being rooted and grounded in love, may have strength to comprehend with all the saints what is the breadth and length and height and depth, and to know the love of Christ that surpasses knowledge, that you may be filled with all the fullness of God. (Ephesians 3:17–19)

So we have come to know and to believe the love that God has for us. God is love, and whoever abides in love abides in God, and God abides in him. (1 John 4:16)

John 18
Broken, Part 1

*Then Pilate said to him, "So you are a king?" Jesus
answered, "You say that I am a king. For this purpose
I was born and for this purpose I have come into the
world—to bear witness to the truth. Everyone who is of
the truth listens to my voice."*

—John 18:37

Have you ever said something you wanted to retract or done
something you wanted to undo? Let's face it, if you're human, you
have at some point said or done something you regretted. We all
have. I remember saying hurtful things when I was young and
selfish, and I remember saying hurtful things when I was not so
young and still selfish. And conversely, I've been on the receiving
end of hurtful words. Both scenarios result in pain. Because of
the enemy, the struggle to overcome our sinful nature is continuous and rages on no matter our age or stage in life. I recently
heard someone say they'd quit wondering if people were good or
bad because honestly, everyone is both.

In John 18, we move into a scene fraught with tension. After
praying such powerful words of love over His disciples, Jesus
left the upper room and went across a brook called Kidron into
an olive grove known as the Garden of Gethsemane (v. 1). His
loyal disciples followed along, probably noticing the change in
His demeanor as they walked beside their teacher and friend.

Led by Judas, the disciple who betrayed Jesus, a band of soldiers also appeared in the garden. Stepping forward Jesus responded, "I told you that I am He. So, if you seek me, let these men go" (v. 8). Of course, Jesus wanted to protect those He loved and spare them from pain. "This was to fulfill the word that he had spoken: 'Of those whom you gave me I have lost not one'" (v. 9).

At this point, John shifts our focus toward Peter. Jesus had proved Himself to Peter time and again through many miracles, but on this night, Peter's fear overcame his faith. As animosity rose in the garden and the soldiers threatened his Lord, Peter drew his sword in defense and slashed off the high priest's servant's ear. Jesus immediately told Peter to put away the sword, reminding him that the events unfolding were accomplishing God's plan (vv. 10–11). But as the night wore on, and Jesus was apprehended by His enemies, Peter's fear took control, and he folded.

Jesus was taken by the soldiers to Annas, the father-in-law of the high priest, who questioned Him. Next He was led into a courtyard before the high priest, Caiaphas, for more questions. Here we see Peter afraid for his life—so afraid, in fact, that he ultimately denied, denied, and denied again even knowing His beloved Jesus. When the long night was over and the cock crowed as Jesus had predicted the night before at the Last Supper, Peter remembered what Jesus had said, and he went out and wept bitterly (Matthew 26:75). Peter had failed the test, as we often do. Peter's heart broke, as ours often does after we fail. He was ashamed. He crumbled. As described in the gospels of Matthew and Luke, Peter wept bitterly. Can you imagine his sorrow? It must have been almost too much to bear.

After appearing before the high priest, Jesus was taken to the governor's headquarters where Pontius Pilate, the fifth governor of the province of Judaea, took over. Those with the power to judge and sentence Jesus continued with their questions. At this point, no one had accused Him of any crime. They must have been extremely conflicted. The Jewish leaders, threatened to their core, hated Jesus and everything He represented, and they wanted to be rid of Him. But what crime had He committed? After a third round of questioning, Pilate reported to the angry Jews, "I find no guilt in him" (v. 38). But the people's irate shouts prevailed, and Pilate made up his mind to let the crowd decide. "But you have a custom that I should release one man for you at the Passover. So do you want me to release to you the King of the Jews?" (v. 39). It seemed Pilate had hoped that the people would want to punish the true criminal. But in the end, his plan backfired. The crowd chose a robber to release and Jesus to die.

As Jesus approached the final and most important charge for which His Father had sent Him to earth, we can be assured that His strength came from God. He knew He was not alone. "Jesus answered, 'You say that I am a king. For this purpose I was born and for this purpose I have come into the world—to bear witness to the truth. Everyone who is of the truth listens to my voice'" (v. 37). He stood on a solid platform of truth. He knew His Father loved Him and that His story would result in salvation for all believers.

You and I, like Peter, sometimes feel separated from God because of our sin and shame. But God is never far off. He is always ready to receive us. We turn away, He pulls us back. We run from Him, and when we're *broken* and ready to return, He's there, waiting with love and acceptance.

When we resist Him, it most certainly brings Him pain, but praise God, He never turns away from us. In fact, because He is a God defined by grace, He loves us even more than we can ever imagine. He will never hold our past against us. He only wants us to repent. He so longs for our return. Open your heart to Him today. He is expecting you.

Promise

Therefore the LORD waits to be gracious to you,
    and therefore he exalts himself to show mercy to you.
For the LORD is a God of justice;
    blessed are all those who wait for him. (Isaiah 30:18)

John 18
Broken, Part 2

In John 18, emotions were raw. The disciples' inability to stay awake in the garden brought intense grief. Peter's denial of Christ brought intense heartache and shame. Jesus surely felt unimaginable dread as He faced intense persecution and death. But He was able to move forward, trusting His Father despite the tension surrounding Him. How was He able to face what lay ahead? God provided the strength He needed to endure the upcoming hours, and Jesus trusted Him. He trusted that these horrendous days of torture would soon pass and, as a result, that God's people would be saved.

Process
1. Do you sometimes feel the inability to press through tough times?
2. Do you feel ashamed that you are questioning God?
3. How would you define grace?
4. Think of a time in your life when you felt broken. Stop and consider that Jesus was grieving with and for you and He always knows how you feel.
5. How was Jesus able to have strength in the face of His persecution and death? How can you apply this to the challenges of your own life?

Prayer

Like Peter, I sometimes feel separated from You because of my failure. Thank You, God, that You are never far away. Thank You that You will never leave me, no matter what I do. Thank You that because of Your grace, You receive me time and again. It's hard for me to believe that when I turn away, You are always there to pull me back. No matter how broken I am, You are there to heal me. When I resist You, I know that it breaks Your heart, but still You never turn away from me. Thank You for never holding my past against me. Help me to repent and regularly reunite with You. Thank You that Your heart and arms are always open to me.

Promises

The LORD is good to those who wait for him,
   to the soul who seeks him.
It is good that one should wait quietly
   for the salvation of the LORD. (Lamentations 3:25–26)

It will be said on that day,
   "Behold, this is our God; we have waited for him, that he might save us.
   This is the LORD; we have waited for him;
   let us be glad and rejoice in his salvation." (Isaiah 25:9)

Oh, taste and see that the LORD is good!
   Blessed is the man who takes refuge in him! (Psalm 34:8)

John 19
Pardoned, Part 1

"It is finished," and he bowed his head and gave up his spirit.

—John 19:30

Not long ago, a change of governmental leadership took place in our country. During the transfer of power from one president to the next, I heard an interesting story on the news. The story explained that traditionally in our nation's history, this particular day has been considered the day of pardon. Our president has been given authority by the Constitution to grant federal pardons, that is, to set aside the punishment for someone who has been convicted of a federal crime. It also explained the tradition that the president waits until the proverbial last hour of his presidency to issue these pardons.

Presidential pardons always draw criticism from the opposite political party, affecting the president's reputation going forward. That day, as I listened to the list of people who were to be granted clemency, I was astounded. These people would be released from prison and home in time for dinner. Can you imagine? One day they are incarcerated, and the next, they are sitting in a lounge chair enjoying a cocktail. The president receives thousands of letters from people pleading for the release of their loved ones. Of all our presidents, Franklin D. Roosevelt granted the most presidential pardons: 2,819.[1] As I listened to the news, I was reminded of and deeply moved by the pardon that has been granted to us by God through His Son, Jesus. This pardon is called grace. Let's look at the parallels in John 19 and embrace a spirit of gratitude that we are no longer trapped behind bars of steel, imprisoned by our sin. Instead, because of Jesus, we are free.

The stories in this chapter are emotionally painful to process. Agony and shame were cast mercilessly upon Jesus. He was ridiculed, flogged, beaten, and ultimately put to a horrendous death by crucifixion on a cross. For those who believed God had sent Jesus to save them, these hours were unbearable as all hope seemed lost. For those who did not believe Jesus was the Messiah, the torture inflicted upon Him was entertainment and revenge. They reveled in the painful punishment for this liar, this lunatic who had disrupted their religion with a radical message. They jeered at and mocked Him. They celebrated His demise.

One of the key figures in this chapter is Governor Pontius Pilate, whom we met in chapter 18. Jesus's life was in his hands. He had the power to clear His record and release Jesus or declare His guilt and have Him killed. In this passage, Pilate's internal conflict was intense. The decision before him was monumental. He held all the power and all the responsibility. It seems he might have believed that Jesus was indeed who He claimed to be. "I find no guilt in Him," Pilate said in verse 6. But popular opinion and a disruptive crowd threatening a riot swayed him, and he turned Jesus over to the people, allowing them to decide His fate. "So he delivered Him over to them to be crucified" (v. 16). Then Pilate did something interesting, something that revealed his inner

---

[1] "Clemency Statistics," The United States Department of Justice, https://www.justice.gov/pardon/clemency-statistics#fdr.

thoughts. "Pilate also wrote an inscription and put it on the cross. It read, 'Jesus of Nazareth, the King of the Jews'" (v. 19). The chief priests of the Jews took issue. They said "Do not write, 'The King of the Jews,' but rather, 'This man said, I am King of the Jews'" (v. 21). And how did Pilate respond? "What I have written I have written" (v. 22). Pilate knew the truth: Jesus was the true King.

As He took His last earthly breath, Jesus said, "It is finished" (v. 30).

It's impossible to imagine what Jesus went through or how He felt. Unjustly accused and convicted, He experienced a horrific death. Although Jesus was God, the Bible tells us that while He lived in human form, he felt human pain, both emotional and physical (Isaiah 53:5). Why would God allow His Son to go through this horrible end to His time on earth? He did it for us. He did it so that we would not have to. He did it because He loves us and wants to save us since we belong to Him. "For our sake he made him to be sin who knew no sin, so that in him we might become the righteousness of God" (2 Corinthians 5:21). God sent His Son to be the ultimate and final sacrifice for our sin. He allowed His Son to suffer to the point of death so that we can live guilt free. He took our blemished record and wiped it clean. Our shortcomings and failures are replaced by His perfection.

The story of Jesus's death at Easter might have become so familiar to some of us that it no longer impacts us as it did the first time we heard it. Maybe, since many of us have heard it time and time again, it doesn't fully grip our hearts. So how do we continue to feel the power of Jesus's crucifixion and allow God's grace to deeply impact us? The answer comes by receiving the ultimate gift that Jesus gave, His life, which is beyond comprehension. In plain terms, we've been given a get-out-of-jail-free card. We get to proceed without being punished, because of Him. And all He asks of us is that we simply believe in Him.

This gift of grace is a gift that keeps on giving. The debt for our sin has been paid once and for all. We've been pardoned. Our punishment has been set aside. We will never be tried again. "It is finished," Jesus said in verse 30. Not only was Jesus's life and purpose on earth finished but also the old way of having to adhere to religious rituals was finished. God was revealing His grace in a way that humanity had never known! As a result of Jesus's death, we have been *pardoned*. We are relieved of guilt, and although we did nothing to deserve this pardon, it has been granted. Because of His faithfulness, we are fully forgiven and forever free.

Promise

If we confess our sins, he is faithful and just to forgive us our sins and to cleanse us from all unrighteousness. (1 John 1:9)

John 19
Pardoned, Part 2

As we enter the final chapters in the book of John, we are reminded of and deeply moved by the pardon that has been granted to us by God through the death and resurrection of His Son, Jesus Christ. This pardon provides grace and is free. When we truly understand that we are no longer imprisoned by our sin, we will begin to gain a desire to live freely for our Savior and King. May we always remember the agony and shame He endured on our behalf. He died so that we could freely live. The old religious ways have passed, and we are invited into a life-changing, warm relationship with a God who loves us unconditionally. Because of His faithfulness, we are forgiven and forever free.

Process
1. Write a short prayer asking God to give you a new perspective on the age-old story of Easter.
2. As you read through John 19, put yourself in Jesus's place. What emotions arise in your soul?
3. Express gratitude that Jesus went to the cross, enduring pain and shame on your behalf.
4. For which of your failures are you most grateful to receive forgiveness today?
5. How does a fresh understanding of grace motivate you to live for Jesus?

Prayer

Thank You, Father God, for sending Your Son, Jesus, as the ultimate and final sacrifice for my sin. I can't imagine that You would allow Your Son to suffer to the point of death so that I can live free of guilt and shame. Fill me with gratitude for this beautiful and unimaginable gift. Because of Your faithfulness, I am forgiven. Thank You, Jesus, for the words You spoke on the cross—"It is finished"—which represent the grace You offer for everyone who trusts in You as their Savior. Help me to daily feel the impact of Your crucifixion and allow Your forgiveness to deeply affect me. Once again, as I acknowledge the ultimate gift of freedom for my soul, help me always remember what You have done for me.

Promises

I will cleanse them from all the guilt of their sin against me, and I will forgive all the guilt of their sin and rebellion against me. (Jeremiah 33:8)

I acknowledged my sin to you,
    and I did not cover my iniquity;
I said, "I will confess my transgressions to the LORD,"
    and you forgave the iniquity of my sin. (Psalm 32:5)

But if we walk in the light, as he is in the light, we have fellowship with one another, and the blood of Jesus his Son cleanses us from all sin. (1 John 1:7)

John 20
Glad, Part 1

When he had said this, he showed them his hands and his side. Then the disciples were glad when they saw the Lord.

—John 20:20

Long ago during wartime and before modern technology, families would wait days, weeks, or even months to hear the fate of their beloved soldiers. Crowds would gather in town squares or near newspaper or telegraph offices for word from the front lines. Sometimes, especially after battles, casualty lists were posted or read aloud, bringing news of the injured and the dead. The anticipation and arrival of these lists brought dread, anxiety, and too often deep pain.

But word did not always make it back home from the battlefields. Sometimes unannounced, a soldier would walk through the door, alive and well. Family members, overjoyed and shocked, would embrace the one they feared dead as their loved one returned in the flesh. What unimaginable relief and elation this must have brought.

John 20 opens on the third day after Jesus's death. Early in the morning before the sun has risen, we find Mary Magdalene approaching the tomb where Jesus has been laid. And what does she find? Stunned, she sees an opened and empty tomb. Horrified that someone has taken Jesus's body, she hurries to tell Peter and John.

Peter and John immediately head to the tomb in a footrace that John wins. Upon arrival, they enter and find empty grave clothes and Jesus's body gone. It's likely at this moment that a small seed of hope is planted in their hearts. But we're told they did not yet understand (v. 9), and they head back home. Mary Magdalene is left alone at the empty tomb, weeping.

And then the most astounding thing occurs. Two angels appear inside the empty tomb and ask Mary why she is weeping (vv. 12–13). Maybe Mary is so overcome with emotion that she doesn't realize they are angels, or maybe she does, but she answers through her tears, "They have taken away my Lord, and I do not know where they have laid him." What happens next will take your breath away. Mary turns around, and although she doesn't know it, she sees Jesus. The one she loves so dearly, the one who has been put to death only days before, stands in her presence, a living breathing human and an all-powerful God. When He speaks her name, she knows. She understands. Her Lord, her Messiah, the Son of God, has truly risen from the dead. He has accomplished exactly what He promised.

He is alive.

Mary quickly shares the astounding news with the disciples. That night, they gather together—everyone except Thomas— locked inside "for fear of the Jews" (v. 19). Suddenly, Jesus miraculously appears among them. He says, "Peace be with you." Imagine how they must have felt, their beloved teacher and friend who they'd witnessed die a horrific death, alive and well standing in front of them, offering His scars as proof. We're told they were *glad*, but they were likely also amazed and maybe even speechless. Jesus continues to speak and says again, "Peace be with you. As the Father has sent me, even so I am sending you" (v. 21). Then something else inconceivable happens. Jesus breathes the Holy Spirit upon them. What a rush that must have been. He has come back, temporarily, to commission them to spread the wonderful news of His resurrection to others, but He is not sending them out alone. He is providing assistance in the form of the Holy Spirit. Things finally begin to make sense. Everything has happened just as He said it would. Jesus's time had come, and now, so has theirs.

Later, when the disciples tell Thomas they've seen Jesus, he does not believe them. In fact, he says he'll never believe that Jesus has risen from the dead unless he sees His scars with his own eyes and feels them with his own hands. Eight days later, he has that opportunity. The group, this time including Thomas, is once again locked inside together when Jesus appears for a second time among them. Now Thomas has the opportunity to witness his risen Savior firsthand, scars clearly visible, and this time, he believes. "My Lord and my God!" he exclaims, likely falling to his knees before his risen Savior (v. 28).

Maybe we can relate to Thomas today, having never seen Jesus in the flesh. He says, "Have you believed because you have seen me? Blessed are those who have not seen and yet have believed" (v. 29). Jesus knew there would be so many of us who would never see His scars in a physical sense, but still we are asked to believe. We are asked to have faith in a God upon whom we cannot rest our eyes. We are asked to place trust in One whom we can't physically touch or hear or smell. He doesn't say it will be easy. And at times, it isn't. Sometimes you'll feel He's not there, that He's left you alone. But if you believe in Him, He is with you, always. He never leaves you. He's there even when your life seems out of control. Can you believe that? Can you trust Him? If you do, at times life might prove overwhelming, and it also might become challenging to accept and remember your new identity—your acceptance into the family of God. But if you do trust in Him as His child, you will be provided a way to move forward with more peace through tough times. The Holy Spirit, God's Holy Spirit, ensures it.

As we hear the narrative of the Easter story and its astonishing conclusion, it truly can be hard to believe. But like a returning soldier who was assumed dead, Jesus, because of His Father, miraculously returned to life. The empty tomb seems to echo the message: you are a new person, loved, forgiven, and secure in the family of God. If you believe, your life will be different not just on Easter Sunday, but on every single day of the year. The resurrection of Jesus changes everything.

Promise
The LORD your God is in your midst,
    a mighty one who will save;
he will rejoice over you with gladness;
    he will quiet you by his love;
he will exult over you with loud singing. (Zephaniah 3:17)

John 20
Glad, Part 2

"He is alive!" The first people to find the tomb empty surely must have felt stunned and astonished. Everything Jesus had told them had come true, and it all finally made sense. The Messiah, the Son of God, had truly risen from the dead and conquered sin. Jesus had accomplished exactly what He promised. His resurrection changed everything, for them and for us. John tells us that the people were glad, and we, too, will be immensely glad when we believe His promises. Jesus offered the powerful and peaceful presence of His Spirit to His followers just as He offers to us today. This was an astonishing conclusion, one that seemed almost too good to be true. As you think about the empty tomb, remember that you are forgiven and free! You are a new person, a beloved part of the family of God. Because of Him, our lives will be different not only on Easter but also on every single day of the year.

Process
1. Why is it sometimes so hard to believe that God is good and has a purposeful plan for your life?
2. What emotions bubble up when you forget that your identity and worth is in Christ?
3. What lies about yourself repeat themselves in your head?
4. What is one practical thing you could do to remind yourself about how God sees you?
5. How does Easter and the resurrection change everything for you personally?

Prayer

Dear Lord, as I focus on the resurrection and have faith in You, give me a newfound strength to believe. Open my eyes to a new way of living, free from guilt, because of You. Sometimes I find it so difficult to trust You. Help me to believe that You're always with me even when life seems out of control. Help me to remember that my worth is defined by You. May my identity be wrapped in Your acceptance and love for me. Help me have the strength to move forward with security and peace, believing that I'm a part of Your family. I put my trust in You, the One who has saved me. Truly, Your resurrection has changed me!

Promises

You make known to me the path of life;
in your presence there is fullness of joy;
at your right hand are pleasures forevermore. (Psalm 16:11)

Consequently, he is able to save to the uttermost those who draw near to God through him, since he always lives to make intercession for them. (Hebrews 7:25)

The LORD has taken away the judgments against you;
he has cleared away your enemies.
The King of Israel, the LORD, is in your midst;
you shall never again fear evil. (Zephaniah 3:15)

John 21
Free, Part 1

Jesus said to them, "Come and have breakfast." Now none of the disciples dared ask him, "Who are you?" They knew it was the Lord.

—John 21:12

One night not long after Jesus's first two appearances to His disciples, Peter decided to go fishing in the Sea of Tiberias. Several of the other disciples—Thomas, Nathanael, James and John, and a couple others—offered to go along (vv. 1–3). Surely their thoughts revolved around Jesus. They had now seen their risen Savior in the flesh twice since the resurrection. With each appearance, Jesus drove the nail of belief deeper into their hearts. They now had clear evidence that everything Jesus had predicted had come true. Can you imagine the atmosphere of reverence as they pondered what had taken place over the last few days? If ever they would believe, the time was now. At daybreak, after the disciples had fished all night with no success, Jesus showed Himself to them, tenderly receiving them for a third time.

John's narrative is about to close as Jesus's time on earth nears its end. Here we once again see Jesus use fishing to illustrate a principle. The disciples' nets remained empty after the long night's work. He knew they were likely frustrated. But the most amazing fishing guide ever sees them from the shore and asks them if they've caught any fish (v. 5). When they respond no, He tells them to cast their net on the right side of the boat. Having heard this same suggestion when they first met Jesus (Luke 5:4), it surely resonated, because as soon as John saw the fish, he said, "It is the Lord!" (John 21:7). As Jesus looked on from the beach, He must have been amused watching them struggle to pull in their net filled with 153 large fish. His time with the disciples had come full circle. He'd begun the journey with a miraculous net full of fish, and now, He was ending it in the same way. While they hadn't fully understood the illustration the first time, now it became clear. Jesus didn't even have to explain in words. They knew with the help of the Holy Spirit, they were to be fishers for the souls of men, clearly showing others the way to salvation.

Someone recently told me about an interesting conversation. Those involved were asked, "What would you say are the most important words for one person to hear from another?" Of course, the first statement people wanted to hear was, "I love you." The second statement people wanted to hear was, "I forgive you." But what came third? This isn't quite as easy to predict. Surprisingly, the overwhelming response was, "Will you come and eat with me?" What a welcoming and tender question. Obviously we would want to share a meal with someone for whom we care, with whom we feel comfortable, or by whom we feel accepted.

Jesus said to the disciples after they caught the fish, "Come and have breakfast" (v. 12). In other words, "Will you come and eat with me?" This invitation included some of the last words this band of brothers heard before Jesus ascended to heaven. They must have been glad as they smelled the enticing aroma of fish roasting on the beachside fire. Jesus knew they were hungry, and He nourished them yet again, just as He had served and honored them so many times before. They would never forget the taste of His provision, even long after He was gone.

The time for which He had prepared them was at hand, and He would soon be departing. With this third appearance, they must have wondered if it was the last. As we listen to the fireside conversation, let's cling to the words spoken by the risen Lord in this last chapter of John. Just like we remember the last words of a loved one before they depart this earth, let's consider the words Jesus chose upon His departure. What were the most important truths for Him to communicate in this last hour?

After Jesus had served them breakfast, He spoke to them with imagery, as He had done so many times before. Jesus transitioned from fish to lambs, instructing His team with urgency. He spoke directly to Simon Peter as the others listened in (v. 15). His question, three times: "Do you love me?" (vv. 15, 16, 17). And Peter's response? A resounding yes. How precious that Jesus offered Peter a chance to redeem himself. Peter's three-time denial on the night of Jesus's arrest was overridden by his three-time proclamation of love for his Savior. How beautifully kind and forgiving of Him to leave Peter with this opportunity for redemption.

Jesus then told Peter and the others, "feed my lambs" and "tend my sheep." So what exactly did Jesus mean by this? Matthew penned what we call the Great Commission in the last chapter of his gospel, explaining what Jesus meant with His analogy. "Go therefore and make disciples of all nations, baptizing them in the name of the Father and of the Son and of the Holy Spirit, teaching them to observe all that I have commanded you. And behold, I am with you always, to the end of the age" (Matthew 28:19–20). This was their commission: to minister to the flocks of people with whom they would engage in the coming days, months, and years. Jesus had been the ultimate example of the perfect shepherd. He had accomplished the work of God His Father. "I glorified you on earth, having accomplished the work that you gave me to do" (John 17:4). The disciples had witnessed Jesus reach out to a world in need. They had traveled with Him, shared meals with Him, and witnessed many miracles performed by Him. After having watched Him anoint so many with physical and spiritual healing, their faith had grown strong. Now it was time for them to accomplish His plan, just as He had accomplished His Father's plans. As He fed them fish and bread on the beach, He called them to go out and feed others. He had nurtured them, and now it was their turn to go out and nurture others.

John's story about Jesus's time on earth has ended. The last verse in the book of John convinces and compels us as we move forward in life. "Now there are also many other things that Jesus did. Were every one of them to be written, I suppose that the world itself could not contain the books that would be written" (v. 25). The stories John chose to include in his gospel lead us straight to our new identity as children in the family of God, *free* to leave our past behind and to move boldly into a hope-filled future with Him. We are now and evermore defined by what God says about us rather than what we or others believe about us. We are His beloved, forever precious and priceless to Him. May we move forward boldly, believing His words, compelled by the power of His Spirit, and living always for our loving heavenly Father.

Promise
Now the Lord is the Spirit, and where the Spirit of the Lord is, there is freedom. (2 Corinthians 3:17)

John 21
Free, Part 2

Today we find ourselves at the end of Jesus's time on earth. His followers had seen their risen Savior in the flesh. With every appearance, Jesus proved to them that He was alive and that everything He'd foretold had come true. He was filled with tender care for those He loved, those He was about to leave behind. He served them and received them to Himself yet again, and their faith grew stronger. Through all the parables and miracles they had witnessed over time, they had gained a greater understanding of His purpose, and theirs. Now that He was returning to His Father, they would be fueled by the power of the Holy Spirit and have the opportunity to share the news of hope with others. He had extended to them a beautiful invitation into His family, and they were to extend this same invitation to those they would meet in their own lives. We also have the same meaningful opportunity today. If we accept Him, we will receive the power of the Holy Spirit along with the privilege of spreading the amazing news about God and His Son, Jesus. Jesus gave His life for us, saved us, and provided a place for us in His Father's family. It truly makes a difference in who you are and who you will become when you identify with God as your Father and understand the significance of what Jesus did for you on the cross. This is why Easter matters, and this is how the resurrection of Jesus changes you.

Process

1. What is one area of your life where you feel alone or insecure?
2. How can you regularly engage with God in order to be reminded of your identity in Him?
3. What feelings swell within when you realize that Jesus always receives you just as you are?
4. Right now, with gratitude, whisper, "Jesus, I come to You just as I am to receive Your love and grace."
5. What is a new way that you can live out your purpose on earth?

Prayer

Lord Jesus, thank You for revealing Yourself to me through the book of John. Thank You for helping me understand more about how You related to Your people thousands of years ago and how You relate to me today. Help me to be free to leave my past behind and move boldly into a hopeful future with You. I am beyond grateful that I'm forever defined by what You say about me rather than what others say or what I believe about myself. I am beloved, precious and priceless to You. May I believe in Your words and press forward with confidence, compelled by the power of Your Spirit. May I lean into a life of living for and loving You. And on the days that it's hardest for me to believe, remind me once again that because of Your resurrection, I am forever changed.

Promises

And you will know the truth, and the truth will set you free. (John 8:32)

For you did not receive the spirit of slavery to fall back into fear, but you have received the Spirit of adoption as sons, by whom we cry, "Abba! Father!" The Spirit himself bears witness with our spirit that we are children of God. (Romans 8:15–16)

For you were called to freedom, brothers. Only do not use your freedom as an opportunity for the flesh, but through love serve one another. (Galatians 5:13)

Matthew 1
Related

The book of the genealogy of Jesus Christ, the son of David, the son of Abraham. . . . She will bear a son, and you shall call his name Jesus, for he will save his people from their sins.

—Matthew 1:1, 21

The last chapter of John and the first chapter of Matthew are the bookends of the four gospels. Ironically, both of these chapters carry the theme of identity. To find the crowning conclusion of *Easter Matters*, we simply look to Matthew chapter 1, which holds significant meaning when pondering who we are as believers in relation to Christ.

The book of Matthew begins with a lengthy list of names, which makes up the genealogy of Jesus. But let's not skip over or miss the importance of this list that begins with Abraham, follows the line of David, and ends with Jesus. How do the many people in the bloodline of Jesus lead us to look at the theme of identity in Christ once again? Let's take a peek into Matthew's gospel with new focus and through a different lens as we begin by exploring this ancient and important genealogy.

While some of Jesus's forefathers were full of integrity, fearing God and walking in a manner worthy of Him, there are others in His bloodline who were corrupt and had shameful reputations. Jesus's family heritage is riddled with sinners and people who turned their back on God. This list includes murderers, thieves, prostitutes, liars, and rebels. Adam and Eve—the mother and father of all humanity—were deceitful and prideful and turned away from God, convinced they knew better than He. David was a murderer. Judah was a rebel and conspirator. Rahab was a prostitute. Ahaz dismantled the temple and offered sacrifices to other gods. Solomon did evil in the sight of God, living an idolatrous life and marrying against God's commands. God could have chosen upstanding and honorable people for His Son's family tree, but He didn't. It's as if He is telling us that we don't have to measure up to a certain standard to join His family. How humbling to know that God chooses and accepts us just as we are, sin and all, to be His children.

It's unlikely that these sinful relatives of Jesus knew that the Son of God would be born into their family. If they had known, surely they would have been motivated to live more honorable lives in order to represent this family of royalty. If you knew you were a part of Jesus's family, wouldn't that not only give you true significance but also give you more reason to carefully consider what you say and do? Let's bring this closer to home with our identity. If we believe that God is our Father and we understand that we are in the bloodline of Christ, then shouldn't living as adopted children of God change everything about us?

With John as our teacher over the last several weeks, we've learned a new way to understand who we are in relation to Christ. But let's face it, as flawed humans, it's challenging to live continually within this new identity. It's challenging, every day, to remember our connection with Christ and live as a beloved member of His family. So how do we apply the truths we've learned on the most practical level? And how, in a complicated world full of sin, can we daily find our identity in Him? Let's first consider our own lives and then look to Jesus for answers.

We all have many things in life that define us: our families, our jobs, our friends, our health, and so on. It might seem impossible to continually live our lives in light of our relationship to God.

- **Overwhelmed with your job?** Often we are filled with feelings of inadequacy. Those feelings don't define us, but instead, because of Jesus's death and resurrection, we are enough.

- **Struggling with rejection from a loved one?** You are always accepted and loved by God. Return to Him and receive His embrace.

- **Feeling the weight of anxiety?** When you connect with Him, remember that God offers unexplainable peace, and you can trust His plans for your future.

- **Think your life is insignificant?** You are worth so much to Him that He gave His life for you. You are His beloved child.

- **Does the unrest of your country bring fear about the future?** God's promises of protection surround us, and He will redeem all that seems bad in the world.

- **Do you feel insecure because no one seems to notice you?** You can be assured that He sees you and that He cares deeply for you.

- **Is life physically, mentally, or emotionally exhausting?** He promises to make life new and fresh when we lean in to the strength He offers.

- **Does everyone seem to be succeeding in life except you?** Remember that His timing is perfect, even though it doesn't always make sense. He created you like no one else. You are priceless to Him.

- **Financially, do you feel like you never have what you need?** He offers provision in unexpected ways when you look to Him. He will take care of you.
- **Are you ashamed of your addiction and tired of your inability to change?** Remember that He accepts you just as you are and loves you in your brokenness.
- **Have you failed again and again and again?** He pursues you with unconditional loving-kindness every single time you fail.

This is the heavenly Father we worship. And this is what it looks like to celebrate Easter every day.

When struggles continue to come, think back on the words from the book of John that define you.

- Seen
- Priceless
- New
- Known
- Precious
- Nourished
- Validated
- Accepted
- Anointed
- Belonging
- Alive
- Honored
- Served
- Nurtured

- Connected
- Prepared
- Protected
- Broken
- Pardoned
- Glad
- Free

These words describe not only who you are in Jesus but also how to live within your new identity. So what's the secret to truly living in Him despite the ongoing struggles of life? The secret is believing in what God says about us in His Word, trusting in the truth of His character, and walking by faith every day, even when life makes no sense.

As you read Matthew 1, don't forget that Jesus's ancestry is more than a list of names. It's a reminder that, if you believe, you are in the bloodline of Jesus. You are royalty. He has abundant love for you, His child, and His grace cements the relationship as He continues to forgive, accept, and love you no matter who you are or what you've done. This identity, in light of His resurrection, is what we celebrate at Easter. Accept your heavenly Father's invitation to join the family reunion celebration, always remembering that this family is made up of people who desperately need Jesus. This privilege, this opportunity to be in the family of God, *related* to Him, indeed changes everything.

Promise
But when he heard it, he said, "Those who are well have no need of a physician, but those who are sick. Go and learn what this means: 'I desire mercy, and not sacrifice.' For I came not to call the righteous, but sinners." (Matthew 9:12–13)

About the Authors

Anna Nash has a passion for helping people discover God's design for life and work. As a life coach, she focuses on helping people find their God-given purpose. Beacon People, a nonprofit organization, was birthed out of this calling. She is the coauthor of *Christmas Matters: How the Birth of Jesus Makes a Difference Every Day* and the author of *pathFinder: A Journey Towards Purpose* and *wayMaker: To See and Experience God Like Never Before*. Anna is a member of Redeemer Community Church, leads Bible studies, and speaks at women's conferences and workshops around the southeast. She and her husband, Tyler, have four grown children and own Innova Coffee in Birmingham, Alabama. Visit Anna on her website annanash.net.

Katy Shelton graduated with a bachelor of science degree from Auburn University. She is the Amazon best-selling coauthor of *Christmas Matters: How the Birth of Jesus Makes a Difference Every Day* and has been published on blogs, in magazines, and in newspapers. Katy is passionate about all things literary and especially enjoys the challenge of turning an idea into a powerful narrative. Born and raised in Birmingham, Alabama, she now lives south of the city on Lake Martin where she attends Church in the Pines. Katy and her husband, John, have three sons and two daughters-in-law—Sullivan, Drake and Haley, and Jack and Morgan. Visit Katy on her website at katyshelton.com.

Learn more about *Easter Matters* at
https://www.eastermattersbook.com

CPSIA information can be obtained
at www.ICGtesting.com
Printed in the USA
BVHW041019130322
631356BV00014B/860

9 781563 095467